TIM CHESTER
TITUS
FOR YOU

thegoodbook
COMPANY

D1118442

Titus For You

© Tim Chester/The Good Book Company, 2014.
Reprinted 2017, 2021.

Published by:
The Good Book Company

thegoodbook.com | thegoodbook.co.uk
thegoodbook.com.au | thegoodbook.co.nz | thegoodbook.co.in

Unless indicated, all Scripture references are taken from the Holy Bible, New International Version. Copyright © 2011 Biblica. Used by permission.

ISBN: 9781909919600

Printed in India

Design by André Parker

TITUS
FOR YOU

CONTENTS

Series Preface   7

Introduction   9

1. Truth Leading to Godliness *1:1-4*   13

2. Finishing What is Unfinished *1:5-9*   29

3. How Not to Grow in Godliness *1:10-16*   43

4. Living the Good Life *2:1-10*   57

5. Grace and Glory: Appearing and Power *2:11-15*   73

6. Kindness and Renewal *3:3-8a*   89

7. Stress These Things, Live These Things *3:1-2, 8b-15*   103

Glossary   117

Bibliography   121

SERIES PREFACE

Each volume of the *God's Word For You* series takes you to the heart of a book of the Bible, and applies its truths to your heart.

The central aim of each title is to be:

- Bible centred
- Christ glorifying
- Relevantly applied
- Easily readable

You can use *Titus For You:*

To read. You can simply read from cover to cover, as a book that explains and explores the themes, encouragements and challenges of this part of Scripture.

To feed. It can guide you in your own personal regular devotions, or use it alongside a sermon or Bible-study series at your church. Each chapter deals with a section of the Bible book and is divided into two shorter parts, with questions for reflection at the end of each.

To lead. You can use this as a resource to help you teach God's word to others, both in small-group and whole-church settings. You'll find tricky verses or concepts explained using ordinary language, and helpful themes and illustrations along with suggested applications.

These books are not commentaries. They assume no understanding of the original Bible languages, nor a high level of biblical knowledge. Verse references are marked in **bold** so that you can refer to them easily. Any words that are used rarely or differently in everyday language outside the church are marked in grey when they first appear, and are explained in a glossary towards the back. There, you'll also find details of resources you can use alongside this one, in both personal and church life.

Our prayer is that as you read, you'll be struck not by the contents of this book, but by the book it's helping you open up; and that you'll praise not the author of this book, but the One he is pointing you to.

Carl Laferton, Series Editor

INTRODUCTION TO TITUS

It's A Wonderful Life is recognised by the American Film Institute as one of the 100 best American films of all time. It stars James Stewart as George Bailey, a man who in his youth dreamed of travelling the world. But along the way, he's made sacrifices for other people that mean he never got to leave his small town. Now he's a weary, broken man who, through no fault of his own, is going to be declared bankrupt. So he stands on the town bridge, about to commit suicide.

But then his guardian angel intervenes. The angel gives him a vision of what life would have been like if he'd never lived. He sees that his life counts, that it has made a difference. He has truly lived a good life—a wonderful life—touching the lives of many people in small but decisive ways.

In many ways, this is what Paul is doing in the letter he writes to Titus. He is giving us a vision of a life that touches people in small but decisive ways—a life that has eternal consequences. He is setting out the truly good life.

Paul was a man called by God, for the sake of God's people: "a servant of God and an apostle of Jesus Christ to further the faith of God's elect and their knowledge of the truth that leads to godliness" (1:1). His job was to give people a vision of the truth, and to show how that truth will lead to a wonderful life, a life of godliness.

What is that truth? "The hope of eternal life, which God, who does not lie, promised before the beginning of time, and which now at his appointed season he has brought to light through the preaching entrusted to me by the command of God

> This is the truth that brings life and then changes life.

our Saviour" (1:2-3). The truth that creates a good life is the gospel. That is the truth that brings life and then changes life.

And so that is the truth that matters for all of life—in chapter one, Paul warns that those who depart from the gospel become "unfit for doing anything good" (1:16). In chapter two, he underlines that the grace of God teaches us to live godly lives (2:11-12). In chapter three, he tells Titus to stress the gospel so that people "may be careful to devote themselves to doing what is good" (3:8). We are to give one another a vision of the gospel that creates a life of good works, that changes our lives so that we are profitable in God's service.

And this good life overflows into others' lives, too. A gospel-changed life "will make the teaching about God our Saviour attractive" (2:10). The good life is a missional force.

The Setting

Paul and Titus' visit to Crete is not mentioned in Acts; but Titus 1:5 makes clear that they had preached the gospel together, that people had been saved, and that as Paul had moved on he had left Titus behind, in order to appoint elders. Now, some years later (and probably between AD63 and AD65), Paul is writing to encourage Titus to ensure the gospel permeates throughout the church, especially its leaders.

Living the good life of the gospel is always a challenge when we live in a wider culture that defines the good life in other ways. It is particularly hard in a culture where newspapers cannot be trusted and politicians are corrupt; a harsh, selfish, racist culture in which there is a fear of crime; a culture where people are reluctant to do manual work, which is therefore left to migrant workers; a culture in which people routinely overeat.

And that was the culture of first-century Crete: "One of Crete's own prophets has said it: 'Cretans are always liars, evil brutes, lazy gluttons,'" Paul points out (1:12). The quote is from a Cretan philosopher, Epimenides. Epimenides was held in high honour by Cretans—so they could not readily ignore or deny his verdict. And yet, of course, this description of first-century Crete could just as easily be a description of twenty-first century western culture. How do we live as Christians in a dishonest, harsh, selfish culture? How can we survive without adopting those attitudes? How can we live the good life in this situation? These are the questions the letter of Titus addresses, and these are the questions we need help with each day as we seek to live a gospel-changed life in a society that seeks change and finds truth in many places, but so rarely in the gospel.

The Pastoral Letters

Titus is one of three so-called "pastoral epistles" in the New Testament, along with 1 and 2 Timothy, written by Paul to two of his protégés. It is sometimes said that the pastoral epistles represent a shift towards a more organised and regulated form of church life after the breathless vibrancy of the book of Acts. The argument runs that the enthusiasm of the first years of the church was waning and being replaced by a more "grown-up" Christianity. The white-hot evangelistic heat was fading, to be replaced by something more sensible and sustainable. This argument is often used to dismiss the idea that the early church gives us any kind of pattern for the Christian life. The mature model for the church is found in the pastoral epistles, and that model is more institutional than the naive enthusiasm of the early days. Calls to return to enthusiastic evangelism and everyday community life are thus downplayed or dismissed.

This argument makes the pastoral epistles sound boring, as if they were some kind of manual on church administration. Worse still, it makes Christianity after the days of the apostles sound boring. Instead of an energetic gospel movement, we're told we have to operate within a restrained institutionalism.

But the real problem with this argument is that this is not what we find in the book of Acts, nor in the letter of Titus. In Acts, there is a concern for order and organisation, even in the early days of the church. Acts 6 describes the apostles putting structures in place to ensure they can continue focusing on the word of God while also ensuring a proper care for those in need within the church. Structures mattered, even in the early days. But structures were not a replacement for evangelistic zeal. They were designed to promote it: the purpose of handing over the care for the needy was so the apostles could "give our attention to prayer and the ministry of the word" (6:4). The result of these changes was that: "the word of God spread. The number of disciples in Jerusalem increased rapidly, and a large number of priests became obedient to the faith" (v 7).

We find the same concerns in the book of Titus. It is true that Titus has been left in Crete to appoint leaders. But there is no discussion of leadership structures or institutional processes. Instead, it is all about ensuring the gospel is central to the everyday life of the church, so that the world can be reached for Christ. Chapter one is about keeping the gospel central—Titus is to counter false teachers by appointing gospel-centred leaders who can encourage and rebuke with the gospel. Chapter two is about ensuring the gospel is central to everyday life—everyday life is the context both in which the gospel is to be lived and in which it is to be taught. Chapter three is about ensuring the gospel is central for the sake of mission—keeping the gospel central to everyday life so that the world is reached.

> Titus is all about ensuring the gospel is central to the everyday life of the church.

So in Acts we find a concern for organisation to ensure that the gospel mission continues. In Titus, we discover the same concerns. The overriding passion of the first-century believers was to be church in a way that kept the gospel central for life, growth, and mission. Reading Titus in our time will inspire and equip us to make sure our lives and churches do the same.

1. TRUTH LEADING TO GODLINESS

Paul is not a man who wastes words, and in his letter to Titus, his first sentence, which runs from **1:1-3**, is rich in **gospel** truth as it sets before us the goal of **gospel ministry**. **Verse 4** tells us that Paul is writing to Titus, his younger partner whom he has left in Crete, and who has been part of his mission and ministry teams in the past (see Galatians 2:1-3; 2 Corinthians 7:13-16; 8:16-21). Paul describes him as "my true son in our common faith" (Titus **1:4**); verses 1-3 are a description of the faith that they have common; of the "**grace** and peace" that they share.

But who is Paul? "An apostle of Jesus Christ" (**v 1**). Meaning "sent", the word "apostle" is used in two ways in the New Testament. It is used to refer to pioneer church planters. Barnabas, for example, is called an apostle (Acts 14:14). But the more significant and prominent way it is used is to refer to people who were witnesses to Jesus and whose **testimony** is the foundation of the church. These were the twelve **disciples** (with Judas replaced by Matthias in Acts 1:15-26) plus Paul. Paul had not known Jesus when Jesus was on earth, but he had met him on the Damascus Road and received a special calling as the apostle to the **Gentiles**.

In what sense does Paul use the term in Titus 1:1? Probably both. In 1 Corinthians 9:1 he combines both senses: "Am I not free? Am I not an apostle? Have I not seen Jesus our Lord? Are you not the result of my work in the Lord?" Why is Paul called an apostle? For two reasons:

---

* All Titus verse references being looked at in each chapter are in **bold**.
† Words in **grey** are defined in the Glossary (page 117).

he had seen the Lord and he had planted the church in Corinth. Now he writes to Titus, both as the man who had planted the church in Crete and as one of the foundational apostles.

Succession Planning

Paul begins by describing the nature of his apostolic ministry. In one important sense this ministry was unique to the apostles. The testimony provided by the apostles could not be replaced by other people when the apostles died because the next generation had not known Jesus directly. Instead, the apostolic testimony became the New Testament—it was replaced by the written account of their testimony in the Bible.

So the so-called pastoral epistles (1 and 2 Timothy and Titus) are concerned with the issue of succession. Paul has planted churches (in Ephesus and Crete respectively) and is now concerned to ensure leaders take over the care of the church, and that those men are leaders who will be faithful to the gospel message and the gospel task. He is concerned, too, for Timothy and Titus. Why the urgency? Because he knows his ministry is coming to an end: "I have fought the good fight, I have finished the race, I have kept the faith" (2 Timothy 4:7). He needs to prepare Timothy and Titus to take over his pioneering role.

So Paul's description of his ministry in the opening verses of this letter is given to set a model for Titus, for the church in Crete and for all churches throughout history. This perhaps is why he does not begin by describing himself as an apostle—a role unique to his generation and the result of a specific commission from Christ. First and foremost, he describes himself as "a servant of God" (literally *doulos*, slave). The model of ministry described in Titus is a model for all of the servants of God.

> Paul is trying to distil his ministry's essential core.

Paul is looking back and looking forward. He is looking back on his ministry and trying to distil its essential core. And he is looking forward to the ministry of those who will succeed him to give them a pattern to follow. This is what is to be at the heart of gospel ministry—and so this letter provides us with an opportunity to recalibrate our lives and the lives of our churches.

What, then, is that model of ministry that Paul outlines at the beginning of Titus?

The Faith of God's Elect

Paul is a servant and apostle "for the faith of God's elect" (Titus **1:1**, NIV 1984 translation). This could be translated: "according to the faith of God's elect", but it is hard to see what Paul could mean by saying his ministry is based on the faith of other people. It is much more likely to be talking about the *goal* of Paul's ministry; to bring those whom God has chosen to saving faith. He preaches the gospel to everyone, confident that those whom God has chosen (God's elect) will respond with faith.

And faith brings people from real death to real life. Paul tells the Ephesians, and all Christians: "You were dead in your transgressions and sins" (Ephesians 2:1). We were lifeless. We had neither the desire to change, nor the ability to change. Preaching to us was like preaching to a corpse. Imagine seeing a dead man in the street and asking him to improve his life—no matter how persuasive your arguments might be, he would not change. Of course not—he's dead! It is the same with the preaching of the gospel. No matter how persuasive our arguments, people will not turn to God... because they are dead.

Yet this death is not the end of the story: "But because of his great love for us, God, who is rich in mercy, made us alive with Christ even when we were dead in transgressions—it is by grace you have been saved" (2:4-5). We were dead, but God made us alive. He breathed his Spirit into our hearts and gave us new birth. The Spirit gives the desire and the ability to respond to the gospel. Because God has made us alive, we hear the gospel and respond with faith: "For it is by grace you have been saved, through faith—and this is not from yourselves, it is the gift of God—not by works, so that no one can boast" (2:8-9). We are saved by faith. But God has to give us this faith. And he does this by making us alive through the Spirit.

Why are some people saved and not others? Why do some people respond to the gospel with faith and other people reject it? Is it because Christians are more clever or godly or deserving? No, it is all of grace. It is always and only because God chooses to give us life by giving us faith.

This has always been the way God works. In Ezekiel 37, Ezekiel proclaims God's word to a valley of dry bones. The dry bones represent Israel. Israel is dead. They are unable to live for God. Ezekiel preaches and something happens: the bones reconnect and flesh covers them. "But there was no breath in them" (Ezekiel 37:8). They may have looked more human, but they were still dead corpses. It is only when the Ezekiel calls on the breath of God to come that things really change. God's breath (or God's Spirit—it is the same word in Hebrew and Greek) breathes life into the corpses and they become God's people.

Some people think the **sovereignty** of God acts as a disincentive for mission. Why should we preach the gospel if people's responses are ultimately in God's hands? But for Paul it had the opposite effect. He knew there were people out there whom God had chosen to make alive. All they needed was someone to preach the gospel. And he could be that person. If he preached, then those whom God had chosen would put their faith in Christ. It might be a long process, but God would save his elect. All Paul needed to do was preach the gospel.

When Paul first visited Corinth he started, as he normally did, by preaching to the Jews. But, the book of Acts tells us: "they opposed Paul and became abusive" (Acts 18:6). So Paul set up shop next door to the synagogue in someone's house. Many people were saved, but Paul seems to have been discouraged, or weary, or scared. One night the Lord spoke to him in a vision: "Do not be afraid; keep on speaking, do not be silent. For I am with you, and no one is going to attack and harm you, because I have many people in this city" (v 9-10). As a result of this vision, Paul taught God's word in Corinth for a further eighteen months.

What enabled Paul to keep going in the face of threats? It was the knowledge that God had many people in the city. The same is true today. God has many people in your city. His elect are all around you. If you preach the gospel, then God will give them the faith to respond.

I have come to realise that the main thing that stops me witnessing about Christ is the feeling that it will be a waste of time. If I invite my neighbour to an evangelistic event, they will almost certainly say no. If I share the gospel with someone at a party, then they will probably edge away from me. And so I do not bother.

> The main thing that stops me witnessing is the feeling it will be a waste of time.

But this is not how Paul saw his life. His life was lived for the faith of God's elect. God has done the choosing, so God will do the persuading. All Paul had to do was find the elect—and he did that by preaching the gospel to everyone without discrimination.

In my shed I have a tray of seeds. This year I noticed that a number of packets were past their use-by date (I didn't even know seeds had a use-by date!). So I stood there in my shed with these seeds in the palm of my hand. They all looked dead. But perhaps some of them still had the potential for life and growth. There was only one way to find out. I planted them and watered them. Some grew, some didn't. And that is the point, and what made it worthwhile: *some* grew.

It is the same with the people of your city. They look spiritually dead, because they are spiritually dead. But some are God's elect. If you water them by preaching the gospel, then God will use that to bring those people to new life. You cannot tell which are God's elect, but you can preach the gospel.

Think about the people in your city. Think about your neighbours, colleagues and friends. Some may be God's elect. God may grant them life through the Spirit if they hear the gospel. Who are God's elect and who are not? There is only one way to find out.

The Godliness of God's Elect

Paul does not stop working for the faith of God's elect once people are **converted**. The second goal of Paul's ministry is godliness. "Paul, a servant of God and an apostle of Jesus Christ to further the faith of God's elect and their knowledge of the truth that leads to godliness" (Titus **1:1**).

> Paul was not content with people simply coming to faith.

Paul was a great evangelist—but he was not content with people simply coming to faith; he laboured to ensure they would grow in their faith, too. As he puts it in Philippians, his aim is to: "continue with all of you for your progress and joy in the faith" (Philippians 1:25).

The goal of God's servants is the faith of God's elect:

- the beginning of faith—as people become Christians

- the continuation of faith—as people remain Christians

- the progress of faith—as people grow as Christians

- the multiplication of faith—as people themselves become servants for the faith of God's elect

After all, Paul reminds us, truth does not only bring us to God; it leads us into godliness (Titus **1:1**). The link between truth and godliness is ambiguous in the original Greek text. Paul could be talking about the truth that "accords with" godliness (as the ESV suggests). This truth that accords with godliness would be in contrast to other teachings that self-identify as "truths", but do not produce godly lives (this is going to be an issue later in the letter). False teachers are teaching false **doctrine** that leads to corrupts behaviour (v 10-11), whereas there is a conduct that is "appropriate to sound doctrine" (2:1). In this sense godliness **authenticates** the truth; godliness shows that the truth is true. Or, better still, it shows that the truth is living because of the fruit it produces.

Nevertheless, the more natural reading of 1:1 is (as the NIV suggests) that the truth "leads to" godliness. Perhaps it does not matter too much. Is godliness the sign of truth? Or is truth the cause of godliness? The answer, of course, is that both go together. Godliness is the sign of truth because truth leads to godliness.

This pursuit of godliness in people is not separate from Paul's pursuit of faith in people. This is faith bearing fruit. As our faith grows in knowledge, so we will grow in godliness. The more we understand what God has done for us in Christ, the more we will love him and live for him.

Paul will expand on this dynamic in 2:11-12: "For the grace of God has appeared that offers salvation to all people. It teaches us to say 'No' to ungodliness and worldly passions, and to live self-controlled, upright and godly lives in this present age." In 1:1, he says the truth leads to "godliness". In 2:12, the truth leads away from "ungodliness" and towards "godly lives". These three all come from the same Greek root, *eusebeia*.

Paul does not simply want Christians who believe the right things. He did not travel round the Roman world totalling the number of decisions for Christ he had seen in his ministry. His goal was not simply people coming to the front of a meeting to give their lives to Christ. His goal was people whose faith bore fruit in godly living. His goal was not converts, but disciples. For any ministry we are involved in or praying for, that should be our goal, too.

Questions for reflection

1. How does knowing that God does the choosing, and God does the persuading, encourage you to share the gospel? With whom?

2. What difference has knowing the truth of the gospel made to your life this week?

3. Who in your church could you begin to pray for, that they would grow in godliness?

PART TWO

Paul is not simply describing his ministry; he is providing a model for Titus' ministry, and for ministry in every time and place, including ours. So having outlined the goal of his ministry—the faith and godliness of God's elect—next he describes the context and content of this model of gospel ministry.

The Context: From Eternity to Eternity

Paul is an apostle: "to further the faith of God's elect and their knowledge of the truth that leads to godliness—in the hope of eternal life, which God, who does not lie, promised before the beginning of time" (**1:1-2**).

Again, the cause-and-effect is unclear. Does Paul pursue faith and godliness "in hope" ("resting on" hope, as the NIV1984 puts it) or "for hope"? Is hope the starting point or the end point? The answer is probably both. This is a virtuous cycle. Faith leads to hope and hope sustains faith. The more we trust Jesus, the more confident our hope will be. The more confident our hope is, the easier it is to look beyond our present circumstances to trust Jesus.

Paul is setting Christian ministry in its proper context. And what an amazing context it is! It is from eternity, to eternity. What Paul does, and what Titus is to do, and what we do, is set in the context of forever.

The Hope of Eternal Life

What we do reaches forward into the eternal future. We work "in the hope of eternal life" (v 2). What you do today has eternal implications. It bears fruit that will last into eternity.

Christian ministry is like a building project, Paul tells us in 1 Corinthians 3:12-15: "If anyone builds on this foundation [of Jesus Christ] using gold, silver, costly stones, wood, hay or straw, their work will be shown for what it is, because the Day will bring it to light. It will be re-vealed with fire, and the fire will test the quality of each person's work. If what has been built survives, the builder will receive a reward. If it is burned up, the builder will suffer loss but yet will be saved—even though only as one escaping through the flames."

In Sheffield in northern England, where I live, there are buildings that were built with Portland stone and which still look great two hundred years later. Others are made cheaply and have to be replaced after thirty years. Paul urges us to build for the long term—the really long term. He urges us to build with eternity in mind. If we build well by building on the foundation of Jesus Christ (using gold or silver), then our work will last into eternity. But if we build badly (using hay or straw), our work will be consumed by the fires of judgment.

Promised from Before the Beginning of Time

The phrase "eternal life" in Titus **2:2** is literally "the life of the ages". And Paul goes on to say that this eternal life was, literally, "promised before the ages". The word "ages" is the same word (*aios*). This is from eternity to eternity. What we do reaches forward into eternity future—but it also reaches back into eternity past.

> What you do has eternal and divine implications.

What you do has eternal implications. And what you do also has divine implications. It goes right to the heart of God the Father's love for his Son.

Paul says eternal life was "promised before the beginning of time" (v 2). To whom did God make this promise? Who was around to hear a promise made before time began? "He chose us in him before the creation of the world to be holy and blameless in his sight. In love he predestined us for adoption to sonship through Jesus Christ, in accordance with his pleasure and will—to the praise of his glorious grace, which he has freely given us in the One he loves" (Ephesians 1:4-6).

"He chose us in him," says Paul. God the Father chose us in God the Son. God the Father made a promise to his Son. He promised him a bride. He promised him *you*. He did this "in accordance with his pleasure and will". It was his pleasure to choose us. God the Father had such pleasure in his Son that he chose to share that pleasure. He created and recreated us so that we could share his delight in his Son. The Son died so that we could share his experience of sonship and be loved by his Father with the same love that his Son receives.

Paul says something very similar in 2 Timothy 1:8-9: "Join with me in suffering for the gospel, by the power of God. He who has saved us and called us to a holy life—not because of anything we have done but because of his own purpose and grace. This grace was given us in Christ Jesus before the beginning of time." We are saved not because of our merits, but because of God's "purpose and grace". And this grace was given to us before time began "in Christ Jesus". Your faith has eternal implications, and your faith has divine implications. It is the fulfilment of a promise from God the Father to God the Son. The Father sees you and delights in the work of his Son. The Father loves you with the love he has for his Son. The Father chose you so you could share the joy of the triune God.

The same is true of your church. Your church is from eternity to eternity. Nothing is more significant than this. Nothing more important has happened in your town than what has happened in your church (other than what happens in other churches). Nothing.

Early in 2013, space-based telescopes detected the brightest cosmic explosion ever seen. It lit up the stars and hurled radiation across the cosmos. If it had happened within 1,000 light years of earth, it would have destroyed life on our planet. It is the biggest event ever witnessed by human beings.

Except that is not quite true. Someone becoming a Christian is a bigger event. Your conversion was an event that was planned in eternity past and will last into eternity future. A massive cosmic explosion does not compare with the death and resurrection of God's own Son. Conversion is mindblowingly amazing.

And then it gets more amazing.

The Content: Jesus Seen in our Words

How would you complete this sentence? "God, who never lies, promised [the hope of eternal life] before the ages began and at the proper time **manifested** [it] in..." (**1:2-3**, ESV).

Perhaps your answer is *Jesus*: *God has manifested the hope of eternal life in Jesus.* And that is a good answer, a very good answer. It is the answer Paul himself gives later on in this letter to Titus. The term "brought to light" (NIV) or "manifest" has the same root as the word "appeared" in 2:11 and 3:4; and there Paul is talking about Jesus and how he appeared in history, bringing salvation: "For the grace of God has appeared that offers salvation to all people" (2:11); "But when the kindness and love of God our Saviour appeared, he saved us" (3:4-5). Salvation appears in the form of Jesus. God has made his eternal purposes manifest in Jesus.

This is all gloriously true. And that makes what Paul says in **1:3** all the more striking. "At his appointed season he has brought [the hope of eternal life] to light *through the preaching entrusted to me* by the command of God our Saviour."

Eternal life is brought to light in preaching. The eternal promise of God appears when we share the gospel. Eternal life appears in your town when you speak about Jesus.

This is not to say that Paul is saying something different in 1:3 from 2:11 and 3:4. God's purposes are all about Jesus, from eternity past to eternity future. God's plans are brought to light in Jesus. But how is Jesus seen? Where can people see him today? They cannot go to Palestine and see him healing the sick or walking on water. How can they encounter Jesus? In our words, in our evangelism, in our preaching.

As you speak the gospel, eternity enters history. Christ is made present. On a cold day, you can see your breath. It forms a cloud in the air. It is almost as if something like this is happening when we share the gospel. With spiritual eyesight, we see Jesus himself taking shape. He appears and people meet him in our words.

> As you speak the gospel, eternity enters history.

I was speaking on this passage at the twentieth anniversary of a church I helped to plant. Twenty years is not long by UK standards. A few miles from where I live is a church which is 1,000 years old. On the way you pass the remains of an Iron-Age fort which is 2,500 years old. But even these things are but a moment in the context of eternity. Twenty years is nothing.

But those twenty years have been of eternal importance. They have sealed the future of some people for all eternity. A plan God has been devising from before time began came to fruition when those people responded to the gospel with faith.

In AD627, the Northumbrian King Edwin and his counsellors met to discuss how they should respond to the Christian mission of Paulinus. They decided to welcome Christianity, and Edwin was baptised. The eighth-century historian-monk, Bede, describes one of the contributions to the debate:

"Another of the king's chief men signified his agreement with this prudent argument, and went on to say: 'Your Majesty, when we compare the present life of man on earth with that time of which we have no knowledge, it seems to me like the swift flight of a single sparrow through the banqueting-hall where you are sitting at dinner on a winter's day with your thanes and counsellors. In the midst there is comforting fire to warm the hall; outside the storms of winter rain or snow are raging. This sparrow flies swiftly in through one door of the hall, and our through another. While he is inside, he is safe from the winter storms; but after a few minutes of comfort, he vanishes from sight into the wintry world from which he came. Even so, man appears on earth for a little while; but of what went before this life or what follows, we know nothing. Therefore, if this teaching has brought any more certain knowledge, it seems only right that we should follow it."

(*Ecclesiastical History of the English People*,
Book II, Chapter 13, 129-130)

The last twenty years have only been a moment. The next twenty years will be, too—but what a moment! This is a moment when eternal stories will be told and when eternal fates will be sealed. It is a moment when Christ will be shown through our words.

> This is a moment when eternal stories will be told and eternal fates will be sealed.

Verse 1 presented us with God's choice—Paul is God's servant for God's elect. God chooses people; chooses to give them faith in response to the gospel. Without that choice, people remain dead. They hear the gospel, but it does not move them.

But they also remain dead if they do not hear the gospel at all.

So what does God do? First, he chooses people to be saved through the proclamation of the gospel. Second, he commands people to proclaim the gospel to them. Paul says the hope of eternal life has been "brought to light through the preaching *entrusted* to me by the *command* of God our Saviour" (**1:3**). God is a saving God. He gives us the privilege of telling others. He gives us the command to tell others. As we do that, eternity enters history, and Jesus Christ becomes clear.

Questions for reflection

1. How does this passage change your view of your evangelism?

2. How does it change your view of your conversion and identity as a Christian?

3. How does it change your view of, and commitment to, your church?

2. FINISHING WHAT IS UNFINISHED

If you read books about church life or church planting, you will almost certainly read a lot about how to order or structure a church. There is plenty of material presenting a blueprint for good church life. There is still more discussion on how to put on a good event each Sunday morning. What is the best way to organise small groups? What are the best courses for training? What processes do you need to have in place for discipleship? What factors impede growth and how can you overcome them? What administrative systems serve you best as your church grows?

So, given that the reason Paul left Titus in Crete "was that you might put in order what was left unfinished" (**v 5**), we might expect some answers to these kinds of questions in Titus. But none of our questions are addressed in Paul's letter.

Here is Paul giving Titus instructions on how to bring order to the church, but there is nothing on structures, processes or meetings. It is not that these things are unimportant. We need structures and meetings. But they are context-specific. You cannot take a model shaped for one particular place at one particular time and make it a blueprint for every situation. You have to work out these things where you are.

What *is* central and universal—and this is what Paul does focus on—is **discipling** people with the gospel. Paul, it seems, leaves structures, processes and meetings for Titus to work out for himself. What he emphasises throughout this letter is the importance of gospel-centred discipleship. The emphasis is on bringing order by discipling people through the word for mission.

Elders

The immediate application of ordering the church in Crete is the appointment of leaders. That is the implication of the second half of **verse 5**: "The reason I left you in Crete was that you might put in order what was left unfinished and appoint elders in every town, as I directed you." Paul had preached the gospel, founded the church and begun to disciple the new believers. But he had left before he had been able to appoint elders.

We can guess at the reason for that from 1 Timothy, where Paul warns about the danger of appointing people to church leadership too soon. An elder "must not be a recent convert, or he may become conceited and fall under the same judgment as the devil" (1 Timothy 3:6). And so Timothy (and Titus, and Paul himself) should: "not be hasty in the laying on of hands, and do not share in the sins of others ... The sins of some are obvious, reaching the place of judgment ahead of them; the sins of others trail behind them" (1 Timothy 5:22, 24). We need to take time to see people's character—time reveals truths that may not be immediately obvious.

So Paul leaves Titus to continue discipling the believers, with a view to appointing elders. This pattern reflects Paul's own activity on his first missionary journey. He and Barnabas preached the gospel in the cities of Antioch, Iconium, Lystra and Derbe. "Then [some time later] they returned to Lystra, Iconium and Antioch ... Paul and Barnabas appointed elders for them in each church and, with prayer and fasting, committed them to the Lord, in whom they had put their trust" (Acts 14:21, 23).

Notice Paul's missionary strategy for this **pagan** culture. It is to preach the gospel (Titus 1:1-4) and then to organise Christians into local churches (**v 5-9**). His strategy is church planting. He wants to scatter gospel churches throughout the Mediterranean world—and he wants to see elder-led congregations "in every town" (**v 5**). We are meant to ask: is this our passion and aim, too? Are there towns, villages and neighbourhoods without a gospel church? What could your church do to ensure that in ten years, a gospel community is witnessing to Christ in that area?

So ordering the church involves appointing leaders. But, again, it is important to notice that Paul is not concerned to set out particular structures and processes. It is hard, for example, to derive a model of church government from these verses (though some people have tried). Paul's central concern is the character, not the structure, of the leadership team—it is their role, not their hierarchy (**v 9**). So Paul's emphasis when he talks about leadership is identifying good disciples who will make good disciples. He wants leaders who have proved themselves as disciples, and he wants them to spend their time making more disciples.

What do you look for in a leader? We often look for skills—good preaching, a dynamic personality, a pastoral touch, good strategy, administrative capacities. But Paul is much more interested in the type of person they are. If you are a leader in your church or home group, then verses 5-9 show the kind of leader you should be. If you are not a leader, then this is the kind of leader you should expect and (if you have them) enjoy. Pray that your leaders will be people like this.

Blameless in the Home

First, we should expect leaders to be blameless in their home. "An elder must be blameless, faithful to his wife, a man whose children believe and are not open to the charge of being wild and disobedient" (**v 6**). "Blameless" does not mean entirely without fault. No leader is perfect (and leaders and congregations need to remember neither to pretend they are perfect nor demand it). Blameless does mean to have a good reputation, against which an accusation cannot be made.

"Faithful to his wife" simply means a "one-woman man". In other words, this does not exclude single men or (necessarily) men who have remarried. Rather, it means we are to look for men with a strong marriage, who are committed to their wife, who care for their wife, and who have no history of flirting with other women. The same kind of clarification applies to the next phrase: "a man whose children believe". The word "children" here implies small children. Most children in their early years believe what their parents believe. So the beliefs of young children will reflect their home life; and Paul wants to appoint elders whose children's beliefs reflect a home life of Christian faith. As they grow up, they may start to question those beliefs, but in their early years they should reflect the faith of their parents, because their parents are intentionally teaching and modelling faith to them, and exerting loving discipline, rather than allowing their children to be "wild and disobedient". So this does not exclude men whose children have grown up to reject the faith or whose young children are not perfect!

The key issue here is that potential elders must already be leading well in their home. Why? Because "an overseer manages God's household" (**v 7**). The church is God's household—family—and so an elder is managing God's household or family. So the way a man leads his own family will tell you a lot about how he will lead God's family, the church. If he is domineering in his home, he is likely to be domineering in the church. If he fails to take responsibility in his home, he is likely to shirk responsibility in the church. Paul says to Titus: *The most important reference for a church leader is what goes on in his home life.*

Real Men

In the west we have a generation of men who want to live, and are encouraged to live, as perpetual children. It is easy to aim to avoid responsibility rather than bearing it; to follow instead of leading in our homes; to want the benefits of married life while retaining the benefits of singleness. So if we are men, we need to tell ourselves to grow up, and encourage each other to grow up! Our families and our churches need us to lead our families, to take initiative in the church, and to serve in our neighbourhoods. Our families and churches need us to be striving to live like Christ—not to settle for being who we are now but, rather, to step up to who we will one day be.

We need to understand that this is what it means to be a man. It is not about macho posturing. It is about taking responsibility so that others flourish.

So churches need to be training men to be good leaders in their home. That's their key ministry, and that's where the training for church ministry takes place. If you are in some kind of church leadership, are you ensuring your home ministry is godly and committed? If you are aspiring to some kind of church leadership, does your home life suggest you are suited for it?

Blameless in Character

Second, we should look for leaders, and aim to be leaders, who are blameless in their character. In **verse 7**, Paul repeats the word "blameless", but now the focus is on all-round character. Paul lists five negative characteristics to avoid in a potential leader: "not overbearing, not quick-tempered, not given to drunkenness, not violent, not pursuing dishonest gain". Then in **verse 8**, he lists six positive virtues to look for: "hospitable, one who loves what is good, who is self-controlled, upright, holy and disciplined".

Remember, Paul's primary concern is not finding the people with the best skills. His primary concern is with character. We can identify two reasons for this.

First, skills used for selfish ends become destructive. We see this often enough in history. The tyrants of this world do not get where they are simply through luck. They are able people—great orators, charismatic personalities and strategic thinkers. These skills combine to make them effective leaders, who achieve their aims. The problem is not their capabilities, but their characters. Their aims are selfish and bring misery to those they lead. Such extremes may be less common in the church—but it is not unusual for a gifted person to rise quickly only then to crash—and their church crashes with them. Or church leaders use their gifts to maintain their status or expand their empire or settle for a comfortable life—and their church follows their lead and their church's faith **atrophies** with theirs.

Second, failure to teach truth often starts with failure to live morally. A potential overseer must be someone who is not known for "pursuing dishonest gain" (**v 7**). The same word is used in verse 11, where Paul says that false teachers: "must be silenced, because they are disrupting whole households by teaching things they ought not to teach—and that for the sake of dishonest gain". Faulty desires soon enough lead to faulty teaching (1 Timothy 6:3-10).

Faulty desires lead to faulty teaching.

And faulty teaching is attractive if your desires are even slightly wrong—because novelty and controversy sell. Peddling **orthodoxy** is not a great way to make a name for yourself, draw a crowd or sell books, because (by definition!) it has all been said before.

But there is a more significant way in which it is true that false morals lead to false teaching. In Romans 1:18-25, the reason people do not know God is that they "suppress the truth by their wickedness". "Their thinking became futile" because "they neither glorified [God] as God nor gave thanks to him". To put it another way: "they are darkened in their understanding and separated from the life of God because of the ignorance that is in them due to the hardening of their hearts" (Ephesians 4:18). Futile thinking and darkened understanding actually begin with someone not glorifying God, and instead, hardening their heart.

And tragically and dangerously, church leaders are not immune to this. It is possible for leaders to suffer "shipwreck with regard to the faith" (1 Timothy 1:19)—because they have not held onto "a good conscience". In Timothy's context, it was not intellectual doubts or false doctrine that had drawn them away from Christ—it was that they were "eager for money" (6:10). Time and again, those who lose their faith do so because they were first overwhelmed by their passion for power or sex or money. We like to think that we are rational beings who make our moral judgments without bias. But the reality is that we are all prone to justifying our behaviour. We find reasons to do what we want to do. Our desires drive our thinking just as much as our thinking drives our desires. So the question we must ask of any potential leader is this: *what behaviour will they seek to justify?*

This holds for all of us, leaders or not. Truth-failure normally starts with moral-failure. You may not think of yourself as a potential **heretic**. But consider this question: *what behaviour do you instinctively seek to justify? Are there behaviours that you know are sinful, but that you find easy to excuse or belittle so that you can pretend that what is wrong is in fact fine?* It is so easy to seek to change the truth in order to suit our desires; it's much harder, but much healthier, to seek to bring our desires under the control of the truth.

Blameless in Doctrine

Third, we should look for leaders to be blameless in their doctrine. "He must hold firmly to the trustworthy message as it has been taught, so that he can encourage others by sound doctrine and **refute** those who oppose it" (Titus **1:9**). Elders must have the ability to encourage and refute. But even here the emphasis falls not so much on skills, as on holding fast to the truth. It is not so much about an ability to teach, as a passion for the truth.

This is the key way in which elders manage God's family (**v 7**): they "must hold firmly to the trustworthy message as it has been taught, so that [they] can encourage others by sound doctrine and refute those who oppose it" (**v 9**). An elder has two tasks, both of which require him to hold unswervingly to that message. He is to:

- encourage others by sound doctrine

- refute those who oppose it

What does Paul mean by "the trustworthy message"? The same wording is used in 3:8, where Paul speaks of a "trustworthy saying", and so we discover an outline of the message they are told to hold firmly to in 3:3-7: "At one time we too were foolish, disobedient, deceived and enslaved by all kinds of passions and pleasures. We lived in **malice** and envy, being hated and hating one another. But when the kindness and love of God our Saviour appeared, he saved us, not because of righteous things we had done, but because of his mercy. He saved us through the washing of rebirth and renewal by the Holy Spirit, whom he poured out on us generously through Jesus Christ our Saviour, so that, having been justified by his grace, we might become heirs having the hope of eternal life."

It is the **trinitarian** gospel of grace. Paul summarises the love of God the Father, the renewal of God the Spirit and the **redemption** of God the Son. He emphasises that we were are saved "not because of righteous things we had done, but because of his mercy" (3:5).

It is simple, but it is not easy. Leaders must encourage and rebuke their church with the gospel. They must not underplay it, nor say more than it. Their people need them to preach, teach and celebrate the gospel. Their people need them to love, live by and grow in the gospel themselves. They are to be disciples shaped by the gospel (**1:6-8**) and they are to make disciples shaped by the gospel (**v 9**).

What should your leaders be like? Blameless in their home, their character and their doctrine. They need to be disciples who can make disciples.

Questions for reflection

1. How will you pray for your church leader(s)? If you are a church leader, are there any areas of life that need to change?

2. Can you think of times in your life when you've changed what you believe to suit how you want to live? What did it lead to?

3. Are you humble enough to be rebuked? Are you loving enough to give a rebuke?

PART TWO

The sixteenth-century **Reformer** John Calvin said that a church leader:

"ought to have two voices: one, for gathering the sheep; and another, for warding off and driving away wolves and thieves."

(Commentary on Timothy, Titus, Philemon, Titus 1, page 3*)*

Elders need a voice that encourages, and a voice that refutes. Calvin was getting his leadership training straight from Paul: an elder "must hold firmly to the trustworthy message as it has been taught, so that he can encourage others by sound doctrine and refute those who oppose it" (**v 9**).

Paul wants Titus to appoint leaders, but also to model leadership to those leaders. So what kind of model is Titus to set? A quick survey of the verbs used in the commands Paul gives to Titus paints

> Elders need a voice that encourages, and a voice that rebukes.

a clear picture: silence (v 11), rebuke sharply (v 13), teach (2:1, 2, 3, 9, 15), encourage (v 6), encourage and rebuke (v 15), remind (3:1), warn (v 10).

There are two common dangers in pastoral ministry and Paul is alert to both of them. They are what we might call over-pastoring and under-pastoring.

Over-pastoring is what happens when a leader or leaders exercise too much control in the life of a church. They are quick to suppress any dissent and may even end up bullying people. They often personalise issues. Suggestions for change or criticism are responded to in a personal way with counter-accusations. The unconscious aim of such leaders is personal control rather than the maturity of the congregation. This is why Paul says an elder must not be "over-bearing, not quick-tempered" (**1:7**).

Under-pastoring is what happens when a leader or leaders exercise too little leadership within a congregation. They avoid confrontation, so they fail to correct false teaching or challenge ungodly living. They may be good at encouraging people, but weak at rebuking those in error. If the aim of those who over-pastor is personal control, the aim of leaders who under-pastor is personal comfort. They want a quiet life. But Paul says an elder must "refute those who oppose" the gospel (**v 9**) and tells Titus that "rebellious people ... must be silenced" (**v 10-11**).

> The aim of those who under-pastor is a quiet life.

You may not be in leadership. But, as we shall see in Titus 2, we are all called to pastor one another in the church. So we can all have a tendency to over-pastor or under-pastor.

If you think you have a tendency towards over-pastoring or under-pastoring, then the key is not simply to modify your style. The key is to "hold firmly to the trustworthy message as it has been taught" (**v 9**). This is why holding firmly to the gospel is so important.

What is it that drives someone to over-pastor? Proverbs 4:23 says: "Guard your heart above all else, for it determines the course of your life" (NLT). In others words, what shapes our behaviour is the thoughts and desires of our hearts (Mark 7:20-23). Our behaviour goes wrong when our thinking about God and desires for God are misaligned. People over-pastor because they want to feel they are in control, or they are trying to prove themselves through their ministry. They have not embraced the truth that God is great and he is in control; or they have not embraced the truth that God is gracious and their identity is found in Christ. They may believe these truths in theory, but they do not hold them firmly in their *hearts*—and this is revealed in moments of pressure.

What is it that drives someone to under-pastor? People under-pastor because they fear the rejection of other people or crave their approval or they want to be liked (what the Bible calls the "fear of man", Proverbs 29:25). Or they may under-pastor because they want a comfortable life, so they avoid the hard things involved in leadership. They have not embraced the truth that God is the glorious One, who should be feared. Their fear of man is not being eclipsed by the fear of God. Or they have not embraced the truth that the God is good. True and lasting joy is found in him—even in the midst of hard situations.

Leaders need to disciple themselves with the gospel before they can disciple others. That does not mean they need to be perfect—progress rather than perfection is what is required (1 Timothy 4:15). But leaders do need to apply the gospel to their own hearts—otherwise they will be like the hypocrites of whom Jesus warns, who try to take specks out of people's eyes when they have planks in their own eyes (Matthew 7:1-5).

Following Leaders

Paul is not just writing to leaders. The final verse of the letter is significant: "Everyone with me sends you greetings. Greet those who love us in the faith. Grace be with you all" (Titus 3:15). The word "you" in the first half of that verse is singular—Paul is talking to Titus. But the word "you" in the second half is plural; plus Paul adds the word "all"—Paul is talking to the whole church in Crete. In other words, this is a letter to Titus, but Paul expects the church in Crete to overhear what is being said.

So this is, if you like, a public commendation of the work Titus has been given. Paul wants everyone to know that Titus is doing what he has asked him to do. This is probably why Paul starts the letter so formally. He does not need to set out his credentials to Titus, but the church needs to know he speaks as "a servant of God and an apostle of Jesus Christ" (1:1).

So when Paul talks about leaders in this letter, he is describing what everyone in the church should expect leaders to be like, and what you should expect leaders to do. He is saying: *Here is what you should look for in a leader, what you should aspire to as a leader, and what you should pray for for your leaders.*

Encouragement we are good with—we all like encouragement from our leaders. But we do not like the idea of silencing and rebuking so much! We find ourselves thinking: *Who do you think you are? What gives you the right?* These are the great mottos of our age. Our culture is suspicious of authority. But then so was the culture of Crete—they were instinctively "rebellious" (**v 10**). But leaders are to rebuke wrong behaviour and counter false teaching. Silencing, rebuking, teaching, encouraging, warning—do not be surprised if the leaders of your church do these things! It is their God-given job.

But why is this their God-given job? Is Paul some kind of tyrant who just wants everything done his way? No. Paul's driving concern is the "knowledge of the truth that leads to godliness" (v 1). His aim is godliness—people who are like God and who commend God. It is possible to be people who "claim to know God, but by their actions ... deny him" (v 16). You can sound godly, and live godlessly... and end up being literally God-less. A loving leader will put your eternal destiny before your present comfort, and will challenge and rebuke you if they see you treading that path. A loving leader will know that what is nicest for you to hear is not always what is best for you to hear.

> A loving leader will put your eternal destiny before your present comfort.

And for us in the west in the twenty-first century, this is an area of church life which is strongly counter-cultural. We live in a culture that wants to flatten all authority. Most leaders do not relish confrontation. It is the job we all hate doing.

But what I must think about is the people in the church whose walk with God is being disrupted. It is my love for them that makes me go through with it. We need to appreciate and enjoy the leadership God has given us in the church. Trust the leadership of your church. Rest in the structures of the church. They provide a safe place to grow as a Christian.

Hebrews 13:17 says: "Obey your leaders and submit to their authority. They keep watch over you as men who must give an account. Obey them so that their work will be a joy, not a burden, for that would be of no advantage to you" (NIV1984). Our culture immediately wants to ask: *What does it mean to obey?* or: *What are the limits of our submission?* or: *I'm not sure I like them having authority.* But the Christian question to ask is: *How can I make my leaders' work a joy?* It's a great question to ponder when it comes to your pastor(s) or elder(s), and perhaps to actually ask them: *How can I make your work more of a joy?*

Find a Father, Find a Son

In Titus 1:4, Paul describes Titus in a striking way: "My true son in our common faith". In our churches, you often hear people say: *He's a true brother.* And there's nothing wrong with that. But I have never heard someone say: *He's a true father to me* or: *He's my true son.*

Why does this matter? Because the relationship between Titus and Paul, though they are brothers in Christ, is a father-son one. Paul could have said: *Titus, my true brother*, but he chose not to. This is not a relationship of **parity**. It is one in which Paul can command Titus. After all, this is not a letter with some suggestions! Most western secular models of training emphasise the releasing of a person's potential—the approach is one of asking questions rather than imposing answers, and the aim is self-realisation, and so coaches are warned against imposing their ideas on the student.

Paul would not do well in modern secular coaching! He doesn't say to Titus: *I thought you might like to consider saying something in Crete* or: *Here are my thoughts, for what they're worth* or: *What do you think is the best way forward?* No, Paul *directs* Titus—not only because he is an apostle, but because Titus is his "son".

I was talking with Brian Wilson, a church planter in Tasmania, Australia, about the difference between people who succeed in ministry and those who do not. He said that over a lifetime of ministry he has

repeatedly observed that one of the key features of those who succeed is a willingness to seek out the kind of relationship that Paul had
with Timothy and Titus. Effective leaders need a father figure.

There is often a temptation to think that our generation will do better than the previous one, or that we need to stand on our own two
feet. One of the perennial dangers for younger men is the belief that
they know more than they do, or can do more than they can. Or they
know what the Bible says, but do not have the experience to apply
that truth with pastoral sensitivity and power.

If you are a young man with responsibility, then look to an older
man for wisdom—someone who can challenge you. You need him.
Who in your life tells you the hard things you need to hear? To whom
have you given the right to ask you the questions you would rather not
be asked?

> Who in your life tells you the hard things you need to hear?

Often, young people have the energy, while older people have the
wisdom. We need both in the church; and that is why we need one an-
other. Younger people need to press on without despising the wisdom of experience. Older people need to
provide wisdom without quenching the fires of youthful enthusiasm.

Questions for reflection

1. Have you seen or experienced the effects of under-pastoring or
   over-pastoring? If you're in any position of leadership in your
   church, which are you most prone to yourself?

2. When do you find it hardest to submit to your church leadership,
   and why?

3. Do you need to be a spiritual father (or mother), or find a spiritual
   father (or mother)—or both?

3. HOW NOT TO GROW IN GODLINESS

Paul's opening charge to Titus is to "put in order what was left unfinished" (v 5). On the face of it, it is an odd statement. Ordinarily you finish what is unfinished, or you order what is disordered. So why does Paul say that Titus should order what is unfinished?! The answer is that both finishing *and* ordering are needed in Crete—and they both involve the same task.

Paul had preached the gospel, seen converts and formed churches. But he had left before he could "finish" the process by appointing leaders. So Titus has been left to finish what is unfinished, and that means the appointment of leaders. But in the meantime, "rebellious people" have arisen (**v 10**). Disorder has entered the church. So Titus must also order what is disordered. And Paul's solution to a disordered church is the appointment of leaders. Notice the word "for" at the beginning of verse 10. Paul tells Titus to appoint elders *for*—because— there are many rebellious people. The solution for rebellion is… more authority! But this is gospel-centred authority. It is people who disciple others with the gospel. Finishing what is unfinished and ordering what is disordered involves the same task: appointing leaders.

A Disruptive Influence

Why does this matter? Paul gives the reason in **verse 11**: "They must be silenced, because they are disrupting whole households by teaching things they ought not to teach". First-century churches met in homes; and so "disrupting whole households" was Paul's way of referring to the groups who met "in every town" (v 5). Paul is talking about local churches or house groups. So he is not talking about some crazy heretics far away. He is talking about people disrupting the church here in Crete.

Paul appears to have in mind two groups of people. There are those who need to be silenced (**v 11**). But there are also those who have been influenced by what they're saying. So Paul wants Titus to "rebuke" that second group "sharply" (**v 13**), so that they will believe what is "sound", rather than remaining under the influence of those who "reject the truth" (**v 14**). There are some who have utterly rejected the Christian faith, but there are others who are Christians but are being pulled away from the faith. The former need silencing, as far as is possible; the latter need rebuking and calling to **repentance**.

Today, within a local church we often cannot have much impact on outside influences who "reject the truth". But we are to tackle those who are being influenced by them because that influence might ruin "whole households"—families, home groups, even churches. This matters.

Rebellious

The essential problem is people who reject authority and love controversy. "There are many rebellious people, full of meaningless talk and deception, especially those of the circumcision group" (**v 10**). "Rebellious people" is literally "**insubordinate** people". It is the same word that Paul uses in verse 6 to describe the kind of children that would prevent a church appointing a man as an elder. These people are like unruly children. They think they know best and reject authority in the church.

In **verse 12**, Paul calls the Cretans "evil brutes". It is a damning indictment, and probably not something you would want to say of a group of people unless you were able to cite one of their own as the source—which is precisely what Paul is doing here. "One of Crete's own prophets"—the philosopher Epimenides—thinks this of his countrymen. In the Greek language, "Cretan" became a by-word for dishonesty: "to Crete" was to lie.

The phrase translated "evil brutes" is literally "dangerous animals". Crete was famous for having no dangerous animals, but the saying was that the human inhabitants more than made up for this lack of wildlife! Christians are repeatedly described in the Bible as sheep, with Jesus as our Chief Shepherd and church leaders as "under-shepherds" (see 1 Peter 5:1-4). So the problem in Crete is that these Christians do not want to be part of the flock under the shepherd. They want to be like solitary, wild animals. They want to think of themselves individually, not as part of a collective.

But sheep do not do well as wild animals. They need a flock and they need a shepherd. And that holds just as true amid the rampant individualism of western culture today as it did among Cretan society then. Paul's warning to us is this: *Don't be self-willed. Don't be independent. Don't assume you know best. Be willing to sit under authority.* We need other people around us, and we especially need older, more mature Christians to lead us.

Legalistic

We do not know in detail what these false teachers were teaching. Perhaps that is how God intended it, otherwise we could simply dismiss the issues as irrelevant to us, rather than being on guard against people who reject authority and love controversy in whatever form it takes. But one or two things about their teaching are clear.

The people "full of meaningless talk and deception" are "especially those of the circumcision group" (Titus **1:10**). The word "especially" should probably be translated "that is": "There are many rebellious people ... that is, those of the circumcision group". In other words, Paul is not talking about a group within a group (the circumcision group, who are a subset of a wider group of rebellious people)—he is identifying the rebellious people *as* the circumcision group.

We meet the "circumcision group" elsewhere in Paul's ministry. In Galatians 2:12, Paul explains why he had to confront Peter: "Before certain men came from James, he used to eat with the Gentiles. But when they arrived, he began to draw back and separate himself from the Gentiles because he was afraid of those who belonged to the circumcision group." These people said: *You become a Christian by faith in Christ, but to stay a Christian, or grow as a Christian, or to be a good Christian or a proper Christian, you need to be circumcised.* They wanted to make Gentile Christians subject to the Jewish law or some kind of human code of conduct.

This explains Paul's words in Titus **1:14**: Titus is to warn those under the circumcision group's influence so that they "will pay no attention to Jewish myths or to the merely human commands of those who reject the truth". At the very least, it seems they were applying aspects of the law of Moses that had been fulfilled in Jesus to Gentile believers—things like circumcision. But they may also have been adding their own codes of conduct or spiritual disciplines to ensure new believers were kept safe from worldliness and grew in holiness—in other words, "merely human commands" (**v 14**).

Limiting Godliness

When we put **verse 10** alongside **verse 12** as describing those who Titus must silence (**v 11**), there is a surprise. The "circumcision group" (**v 10**) are "liars, evil brutes, lazy gluttons" (**v 12**). This is a general statement about Cretan culture, but Paul says it applies perfectly to the rebellious people who want to insist on the Cretan Christians keeping the whole Jewish ceremonial law, or on them obeying extra rules and commands.

Paul is saying that these religious rules do not enable their followers to escape the influence of the world. Rather, the result of rule-keeping is to completely succumb to it. The circumcision group are being truly Cretan in all the worst ways.

And yet these are not people who are saying: *You can live how you like and throw off all restraint.* No, they are strict, religious people. They are not licentious (live how you want), but legalists (you must live this way). Can legalists be brutes and gluttons? The revolutionary truth of verses 10-12 is that Paul is saying: *Yes, they can.*

How is this? First, because laws and rules that look as if they are about promoting and protecting godliness are actually about limiting godliness. They reduce godliness to ticking some boxes: *As long as I do this, that and the other, then I'm OK* or: *As long as I'm circumcised then I'm godly.* So you can be circumcised and a lying glutton, and yet convince yourself that you

> Laws that look as if they are about promoting godliness are actually about limiting it.

are godly. Being godly becomes being legalistic in several areas of life and ignoring ungodliness in others. So I can convince myself I'm godly because I listen to Christian music and pray, even though I fiddle my timesheets at work, along with everyone else; or because I don't touch alcohol, even though I am short-tempered with my wife; or because I keep the Sabbath extremely strictly, even though I don't give my time on the Sabbath to loving others in my church.

The irony is this: when we react against some aspects of our culture, and set up rules to protect ourselves from them, we ignore other ungodly aspects of that same culture. We limit the demands of godliness, reducing it from becoming Christlike to becoming a little less like our culture in a few ways. Christian maturity is exchanged for not sleeping around, not getting drunk, and turning up to Bible study.

Jesus told the famous story of the good Samaritan in response to a religious expert's question: "Who is my neighbour?" (Luke 10:29). It is a perfectly good question in response to the truth that God's law tells us to: "Love your neighbour as yourself" (v 27). The problem is not the expert's question, but his motivation: "He wanted to justify himself" (v 29). He wanted to know what he needed to do so he could ensure he was good enough for God. What was the minimal requirement that would enable him to inherit eternal life (v 25)? He wanted a specific law to limit what godliness involved. What he got from Jesus was a story that radically expanded the scope of loving your neighbour.

Jesus' point there is what Paul is getting at here: any question about Christian living that begins: *What must I do...?* or ends: *Is that enough?* is born of a legalistic approach that wants to limit godliness, diluting it down from a whole-life commitment to a part-time project.

Let me give you another example. A member of my church rang to ask what he should do, because his friend had asked him to go street-preaching and he did not know how to respond. So the three of us got together. As the conversation began it was clear that the street preaching guy thought we were selling out in some way if we did not join him. But as we talked about sharing our lives with unbelievers, about an evangelism that

> Legalism dilutes godliness from whole-life commitment to part-time project.

was 24/7, about opening our homes, his tone changed. At the end of our conversation he admitted: "I'm not sure if I'm up for that kind of commitment."

His street-preaching routine had looked godly (and it is a good thing to do). But in fact, he wanted a form of evangelism he could stick in his schedule, tick off the list and then switch off. He was not really interested in reaching the lost with the love of Christ. He was just interested in feeling righteous. There is nothing wrong with street preaching—what was wrong was not the action, but this guy's motivation. The story illustrates how easily our grand statements about what Christians ought to do can actually be a front for the ways in which we want to limit what we have to do.

For you it might be another issue. It might be another form of evangelism, or volunteering for the church roster, or reading the Bible every day, or contributing to the church prayer meeting. Of course, all these are right things to do. But we must not make them the measure of godliness, and therefore the limit of godliness. The God who gave us everything at great cost to himself asks for our everything in return. True godliness does not say: *How much must I do?* but rather: *How much can I give?*

Questions for reflection

1. How seriously do you take the issue of divisive teaching?

2. Imagine someone said to you: *I wish our church would give us some clearer rules on how to be godly.* What would you say?

3. Are there ways in which you are tempted to reduce the demands of godly living by turning it into a set of dos and don'ts? How has this chapter challenged you?

PART TWO

Fit for Purpose

A legalist can also be a liar, a brute and/or a glutton because, first, adding rules limits godliness. And, second, because adding rules has no power to change our lives.

We see this all the time, though we are better at seeing it in others than in ourselves. I have known strict, religious people who were evil brutes in the home, bullying their wives. Or teetotallers who could not be trusted with money. It is not sex and drink that corrupt us. We misuse them because our hearts are corrupt—and rules have no power to change hearts.

There is no shortcut to godliness. It is not a matter of pinning up some rules, reading them, and keeping them. Our hearts are sinful, and they cannot manage to produce it. And so creating rules like "Do not handle! Do not taste! Do not touch!", which are based on "human commands and teachings" may "have an appearance of wisdom" but "they lack any value in restraining sensual indulgence" (Colossians 2:21-23).

Paul has already told Titus that it is "knowledge of the truth that leads to godliness" (Titus 1:1). Later, he'll speak of "the grace of God … that offers salvation … teaches us to say 'No' to ungodliness and worldly passions, and to live self-controlled, upright and godly lives in this present age" (2:11-12). Grace is not just for the beginning of the Christian life; it is the fuel for the Christian life.

And legalism is not a substitute fuel. Legalism does not work because it cannot work. It leads to the life of those Paul describes in **1:16**: "They claim to know God, but by their actions they deny him. They are detestable, disobedient and unfit for doing anything good." The false teachers say: *I'm doing what God wants.* But in reality their actions deny him. They have persuaded themselves that they are doing what is right, but their deeds give them away. They are not fit for purpose—for the purpose of "doing … good".

Remember, Paul's ministry to the church has the aim of gospel-truth-based godliness (v 1). Instead of self-willed, self-righteous, selfish people, Paul wants godly people who do good works. This emphasis on God's people being fit for the purpose of doing good runs all the way through the letter (2:11-12, 14; 3:1, 8, 14). The product of Paul's gospel ministry is people who are godly.

And the surprising truth is that the legalistic teachers' product is the opposite: God-denying godlessness. Because legalism limits godliness, and then does not provide the power even to obey the laws it sets, those who promote it and pursue it are "unfit for doing anything good".

We get a sense of what the teaching of the false teachers involved in **1:15**: "To the pure, all things are pure, but to those who are corrupted and do not believe, nothing is pure. In fact, both their minds and consciences are corrupted." It seems some people were saying that if you wanted to be really godly then you should avoid sex (or at least not enjoy it), you should not drink alcohol, and you should only eat simple food. Their essential message was: *You should become like a monk* (except monks had not then been invented!).

Sounds Impressive, Doesn't Work

This kind of teaching always sounds impressive because it seems to reflect a deep concern about worldliness and a radical commitment to holiness. But Paul's assessment of it is damning, on three counts:

1. Rather than being motivated by holiness, it is motivated by "dishonest gain" (**v 11**)—be it financial or reputational.

2. Rather than being about obeying God's will, it is about obeying "merely human commands" (**v 14**).

3. Rather than keeping people pure, it in fact corrupts people (**v 15**).

Paul says they have completely missed the point. If people misuse the good gifts of God's creation (like sex, food and drink) by being, for example, "lazy gluttons" (v 12), then the problem is not with God's good gifts, but with the people concerned. They are the ones who are corrupt, not the sex, food and drink.

Legalism has a long history. Paul's reference to "merely human commands" in **verse 14** is an **allusion** to Jesus' words in Mark 7:7, which themselves are a quote from Isaiah 29:13. Jesus is responding to the Pharisees, who think that sex, alcohol and certain foods are corrupt, and therefore make us corrupt if we consume them. Their religion is outside-in—they locate the problem externally. Jesus turns it the other way around: "Nothing that enters a person from the outside can defile them ... what comes out of a person is what defiles them" (Mark 7:18, 20). Jesus locates the problem internally, in the heart.

> Pharisaical religion is outside-in. Jesus turns it the other way round.

Sex and food are not corrupt. We are the ones who make sex and food corrupt when we use them in sinful and selfish ways. It is not that we are corrupted if we come into contact with sex or food. Rather, sex and food are corrupted when they come into the contact with people with impure hearts! So things like sex, food and drink are pure when we view them as good gifts from God and use them for his glory in accordance with his word (Titus **1:15**).

The true Christian is not to be worldly in the sense of being corrupted by the priorities and values of this world. But we are to enjoy all God's generous provision in this world. Abstaining from his good gifts can be just as corrupt and corrupting as abusing them.

How do we spot this approach, so that we do not fall for it? The late British pastor John Stott suggested that Titus 1 provides us with "three valid tests to apply to any and every system" of thought (in *1 Timothy and Titus*, page 183):

1. Is its origin divine or human, revelation or tradition?

2. Is its essence inward or outward, spiritual or ritual?

3. Is its result a transformed life or a merely formal creed?

True religion is divine in its origin, spiritual in its essence and moral in its effect.

Neither Always Bad, nor Always Good

Consider how these principles might apply to issues we face today. For example, consider the issue of computer games. Someone might argue: *Computer games can be addictive, and can encourage laziness. Therefore computer games are bad.*

Paul would say: *Wrong.* Computer games do not corrupt us. We corrupt computer games because our corrupt hearts use them in addictive ways.

So what should our attitude to computer games be? We cannot say they are always bad and should always be avoided. But neither can we say they are always good and can always be used. If someone is addicted to computer games and is spending time playing games when they should be serving others, or if they are playing long into the night so that their ability to function the following day is impaired, then it may be appropriate for them to get rid of their computer games. But the corrupting influence in this situation is not the computer games, but the user.

Or let us consider another example. Someone might argue: *Romantic comedies encourage people to be discontented. Therefore rom-coms are bad.*

Paul would say: *Wrong.* Romantic comedies do not corrupt us. We corrupt romantic comedies because our corrupt hearts respond with discontentment.

So what should our attitude to romantic comedies be? We cannot say they are always bad and should always be avoided. But neither can we say they are always good and can always be watched. If watching romantic comedies makes you dissatisfied with your singleness or in your marriage, then it may well be appropriate for you to avoid watching them.

Can the same argument be applied to pornography? Could we say: *Pornography does not corrupt us. We corrupt porn only if our corrupt hearts respond to it with lustful thoughts*? No—because porn is *already* a corruption of God's gift of sex. Porn presents corrupt expressions of sex. Even if porn were between a married couple, sex is not intended as a performance, and you are not to be a participant as a voyeur in another couple's sex. We need to distinguish between sex—a good gift that does not corrupt us—and porn—a corruption of that good gift. We corrupt sex because our corrupt hearts distort God's good gift, and one of the ways we corrupt God's good gift of sex is through porn.

You Should Not vs You Need Not

Throughout this opening chapter Paul has been setting up a series of contrasts through the use of repeated words. Bringing these together allows us to see the central thrust of his message:

By the **command** of God our Saviour (v 3)	Merely human **commands** (v 14)
The **truth** that leads to godliness (v 1)	Those who reject the **truth** (v 14)
God, who does not **lie** (v 2)	"Cretans are always **liars**" (v 12)
The truth that **leads to godliness** (v 1)	Their actions ... **deny [God]** (v 16)

A reliance on human commands actually involves a rejection of the truth. That is because the truth is that God "saved us, not because of righteous things we had done, but because of his mercy" (3:5). It is not that we begin the Christian life by grace and then continue or grow through our own efforts. It is that we know and enjoy and appreciate the truth of the gospel—that we are saved by grace at the cross—and as we learn to apply this to our lives, we grow in godliness (1:1).

A helpful way of thinking about the difference is this. Legalism says: *You should not do this.* The gospel says: *You need not do this because God is always bigger and better than sin.* Legalism says: *You should not sleep with your boyfriend... You should read your Bible every day... You should not get drunk... You should witness to your friends... You should not lose your temper.* None of those are good news to someone struggling with those issues. To them, it is condemnation and sounds oppressive. What the gospel says is this: *You need not... You need not get drunk because Jesus offers a better refuge. You need not lose your temper because God is in control of the situation.* Sin is always making promises; and the

> God is bigger and better than anything sin offers.

gospel exposes those promises as false promises and points to God, who is bigger and better than anything sin offers. That is good news.

Unsurprisingly, the gospel approach was Jesus' approach. When he meets a woman at a well in John 4, he knows she has had five husbands and that the man she is now with is not her husband. He could tell her to stop her sexual sin. But instead he offers her living water. She has been looking for meaning, satisfaction and identity in sexual intimacy and not finding it. The arithmetic tells the story: five husbands plus one partner. She has made sexual relationships her saviour, and they have not delivered. Jesus gives her good news by offering meaning, satisfaction and identity in himself. He offers true satisfaction ("living water", v 10) and lasting satisfaction ("welling up to eternal life", v 14). Legalism says: *You should not do this.* The gospel says: *You need not do this because Jesus offers something bigger and better—he offers living water.*

It is not human commands which make disciples. It is the command of God which creates disciples. And what is that command? It is the preaching of the gospel: "the hope of eternal life, which God, who does not lie, promised before the beginning of time, and which now at his appointed season he has brought to light through the preaching entrusted to me by the command of God our Saviour" (Titus 1:2-3).

John Stott said:

"When false teachers increase, [we must] multiply the number of true teachers." (*1 Timothy and Titus*, page 179)

We are all called to commend the gospel to one another so that we live gospel-shaped lives that are fit for purpose—the purpose of doing good. And we will only do this as we learn to live out the gospel, enjoying God's good gifts in a way that brings glory to him and good to us. Legalistic abstention is no more the gospel of grace than licentious abuse is; and running to the first extreme in order to escape the other is to swap one error for another.

Questions for reflection

1. Why does legalism not work in producing godliness?

2. What are the issues you face, or your loved ones face, where you need to find the balance between thinking something is always bad, or always good? What would that balance look like?

3. In what areas do you need to stop saying to yourself: *You should not...* and start reminding yourself: *You need not...*?

4. LIVING THE GOOD LIFE

Paul and Titus had a father-son relationship (1:4). And Paul saw this relationship as vital not only for those in church leadership, but for those in church membership. So now, in chapter 2, he urges Titus to ensure those kinds of discipling relationships are replicated throughout the church.

Chapter one ends with Paul talking about people who "claim to know God, but by their actions ... deny him. They are detestable, disobedient and unfit for doing anything good" (1:16). 2:1 begins: "You, however…" or "But as for you…" (ESV). Chapter two describes what Titus must do in contrast to the self-willed and self-righteous teachers of 1:10-16. His job is to silence false doctrine (v 11)—but it is also to "teach … sound doctrine" (**2:1**). The word "sound" means "healthy". This is teaching that leads to spiritual and emotional health. Titus is to lead his people to a healthy life or a good life, which is characterised by good works.

So what does this good life look like?

A Word for Older Men

Paul gives different instructions for different categories of people—older men, older women, younger women, younger men and slaves. He assumes that different ages and different roles face different challenges and temptations.

Paul begins with "the older men" (**v 2**). Titus needs to teach them "to be temperate, worthy of respect, self-controlled, and sound in faith, in love and in endurance". This suggests their temptations may be to be grumpy, or to pick arguments, or to be cynical, or to be weary of giving themselves in service. Again, the word "sound" literally means "healthy". And it is so unhealthy for our faith, and for the church we're part of, when we give rein to thoughts such as: *This won't work, we tried it before; I don't know why we're bothering; If only things were like they used to be—it wasn't like this in my day.*

Paul says the antidote to this is to be taught faith, love and endurance. Christian men should grow old like Caleb. As a young man, Caleb was one of the twelve spies Moses sent into the land of Canaan. He and Joshua were the only ones who were confident that God could give the Israelites victory, despite the giants in the land—but the others disagreed and Israel did not enter the promised land (Numbers 13 – 14). But the story of Caleb does not end there. Forty-five years later, with Israel now invading Canaan, Caleb is still just as enthusiastic and just as confident in God—even though he is now 85 years old (Joshua 14:6-15). He still wants to be in the middle of the action. He has not retired from serving God.

Younger men in the church need to learn to follow the example of older people. But that is a two-way street. To be able to ask for respect, you need to be "worthy of respect". Older men need to live in such a way that younger guys look at them and think: *I want to be like them.* You do not want them saying: *I hope I don't lose my radical edge like them.*

A Word for Older Women

Older women face similar temptations: "Likewise, teach the older women to be reverent in the way they live, not to be **slanderers** or addicted to much wine, but to teach what is good" (Titus **2:3**).

It's easy for zeal for obedience to wane as we grow older; for "realism" to replace a radical approach to godly living. And it's easy to look down on others: *They're not the wives/mothers/daughters they should be… They don't serve in the church as they should.* Perhaps older women start to worry less about what others think of these kinds of comments, and this "liberates" them to complain and criticise more openly. Paul says: *Instead of complaining about what is wrong, teach about what is good*.

What about younger women? "Then they can urge the younger women to love their husbands and children, to be self-controlled and pure, to be busy at home, to be kind, and to be subject to their husbands, so that no one will malign the word of God" (**v 4-5**). It is not that younger women cannot have a career. But if they are wives and moth-

> Instead of complaining about what is wrong, teach about what is good.

ers, home is the primary place where they are to serve. The call to be "busy at home" is not said just to counter the temptation to be lazy at home, but also to counter the temptation to be over-busy elsewhere—to look for a life beyond the life God has given you.

Young Christian wives should be content with that life. And that is particularly a challenge in our culture, which often despises a domestic life. A review of a new book by the former Political Editor of the British newspaper *The Observer* and now full-time mother, Gaby Hinsliff, said:

"If you do as Hinsliff has done, and hang up your working suits in exchange for an ... apron, the danger is that the once-dynamic 'career mother' can suddenly, and overwhelmingly, be replaced by a woman who feels like a nobody. How very true this is. Hinsliff's description of mums at the school gate who had once 'been somebody and are now mainly somebody's parent' is spot on."

(Rosie Millard, review of *Half a Wife: The Working Family's Guide to Getting a Life Back*, Guardian.co.uk, 6 January 2012)

In our culture, people define themselves by what they do; and especially by their careers. So a woman without a career can feel like "a nobody". But the gospel defines things very differently. If you are someone, or know someone, who defines themselves negatively by what they no longer do, because they are a mother at home, you need to read 2:11-14 alongside 2:4-5. In 2:11-14, Paul says we are Christ's very own people, whom he has redeemed and purified. That is who you are. That is your value. You are Christ's treasured possession. And that identity, given to us through the gospel, liberates us to embrace the often hard, often mundane, but always vital task of looking after children and raising them to know the gospel.

A Word for Young Men

Young men receive only one word of **exhortation**: "Encourage the young men to be self-controlled" (**v 6**). But that does cover the temptations young men face! Lust, ambition, impatience—all require a response of self-control.

Then Paul has a word for Titus himself: "In everything set them an example by doing what is good. In your teaching show integrity, seriousness and soundness of speech that cannot be condemned, so that those who oppose you may be ashamed because they have nothing bad to say about us" (**v 7-8**). The "them" in **verse 7** is a reference to the younger men of **verse 6**. As a young man himself, Titus is to set an example to other young men. These verses then are an amplification of the exhortation to young men. Titus is to set an example of "integrity, seriousness and soundness". Young men need to grow up, to take life seriously, to take their faith seriously and to be responsible. Our society first infantilised the teenage years; now it has done the same for our twenties. There is no room in the church for living for yourself for two or more decades before beginning to live out the biblical picture of a man.

A Word for Workers

Finally there is a word for slaves (or, in our day, employees): "Teach slaves to be subject to their masters in everything, to try to please them, not to talk back to them, and not to steal from them, but to show that they can be fully trusted, so that in every way they will make the teaching about God our Saviour attractive" (**v 9-10**). Paul's exhortations here move us well beyond the kind of legalistic duty Paul warns against in chapter one. Slaves can be subject to masters in a minimal and passive way, doing just what is required and no more. But Paul expands on this by saying they should "try to please them" (**v 9**). This requires so much more than ticking off a checklist of duties. It requires a change of heart, a radically different *attitude*. It requires us to be proactive as we seek to bless our masters.

Paul's words here prompt us to ask ourselves about our own attitudes in our workplace: *Do I merely do the minimum required of me, or do I take the initiative to bless my employers? What would it look like to do that proactively?*

One of the implications of Paul's words to these different groups is obvious but much missed: do not assume that other people should be like you. And do not assume you should be like other people. "Act your age" really is good advice—if what we mean by "act" is informed by the Scriptures. If you are in your twenties, do not live like a child—on your Xbox all the time. It is time to take responsibility in your home, work, church and neighbourhood. If you are in your forties or fifties, do not spend your time wishing you were still young or fit or beautiful. Live life in the present. Enjoy being the age you are, and enjoy contributing in ways that are appropriate for your age.

Self-Control and Submission

As we notice what is different about each of these exhortations, it is also significant to see what is repeated to these different groups. Two things stand out. The first is self-control. Older men, younger women and younger men are all told to be self-controlled:

■ "Teach the older men to be ... self-controlled" (**v 2**)

■ "Urge the younger women ... to be self-controlled" (**v 4-5**)

■ "Similarly, encourage the young men to be self-controlled" (**v 6**)

Verse 6 begins "similarly"; and what is similar about the exhortations to young women and young men is the call to self-control. In 1:8 elders are to be self-controlled. In 2:11-12 we discover where the power to be self-controlled lies: it is "the grace of God [that] teaches us to … live self-controlled, upright and godly lives in this present age". *Everyone* is to be self-controlled.

British people are known for being emotionally repressed—and we even make a virtue of it. But this is not the same as self-control. It is good to feel emotions and to be emotional. We should feel anger, joy or sadness whenever these are the appropriate responses to life. And we should be prepared to show them, when and where it's appropriate.

But we do need to combine emotions with self-control. That is because our emotions can be self-centred. We are called to rejoice with those who rejoice and mourn with those mourn (Romans 12:15). If your joy means you cannot mourn with others or your mourning means you cannot rejoice with others, then your emotions are too self-obsessed—they are not under your control, but rather, they control you.

Or consider the example of anger. The Bible talks about the anger of God (eg: Deuteronomy 6:15; Psalm 74:1; Romans 2:8). Jesus shows anger towards the indifference of religious people (Mark 3:5). So anger can be a good emotion. It is the appropriate response to the evils of sin. God's anger is his measured, settled and consistent opposition to sin. If we are never angry, we are indifferent, and that is not loving.

> If we are never angry, we are not loving.

But often, human anger is distorted. We get angry about the wrong things, or we get angry in the wrong way. Our anger is not self-controlled. Self-controlled anger pursues justice and mercy. Anger without self-control pursues revenge or **catharsis**.

We should not be ruled by our emotions. Emotions are not an excuse to neglect our duties. Be disappointed if another Christian falls away, but do not give up. Be sad if tragedy hits, but do not stay away from your church. Be cross if someone wrongs you, but do not withhold forgiveness. This is self-control—not denying our emotions, but not being controlled by those emotions.

The second common virtue is submission. Titus **2:5** says that young wives are "to be subject to their husbands". **Verse 9** tells Titus to "teach slaves to be subject to their masters in everything, to try to please them, not to talk back to them". In 3:1, Paul will tell Titus to "remind the people to be subject to rulers and authorities, to be obedient".

Paul may be opposing a view that, because Christians are part of the new age of the resurrection, we are now free from the civil and domestic obligations of the present age. We are part of the kingdom of God, and so we no longer have to obey the hierarchies of this passing world. Theologians call this over-realised eschatology. Eschatology is the doctrine of the last days, and the last days have begun in history with the resurrection of Jesus. But Christian hope still looks *forward to*, rather than around at, the redemption and renewal of all things (Romans 8:18-25). Over-realised eschatology expects to see in the present things that actually belong to the return of Christ. So Paul's call to submission may be countering this kind of over-realised eschatology.

Counter-Cultural, yet Compelling

Self-control and submission are profoundly counter-cultural. It was counter-cultural in Crete. We have already seen that "Cretans are always liars, evil brutes, lazy gluttons" (Titus 1:12) These were people who did not control their speech, their emotions or their appetites. It is counter-cultural today. Western culture values self-expression instead of self-control; self-fulfilment instead of self-denial; and independence instead of submission. In fact, self-control and submission have been counter-cultural since the moment Adam and Eve decided to act on their own impulses and desires, and eat the fruit God had commanded them not to.

To be self-controlled and live in right submission will mean swimming against the culture. But it always has done, and so its unpopularity and the **incredulity** of our culture are not legitimate reasons not to do it. People do not like it when they hear Christians talking about self-control and submission. We ourselves often bristle when we read these kinds of calls. And yet Paul says that younger women are "to be subject to their husbands, so that no one will malign the word of God" (**2:5**), and that "slaves [should] be subject to their masters in everything ... so that in every way they will make the teaching about God our Saviour attractive" (**v 9-10**).

Notice the "so that" of submission. This is about cause and effect, and the cause is submission, with the effect of mission. People may not like it when we talk about self-control and submission. But they find it attractive when we live it. Unbelievers who are repelled by Christian teaching on headship within marriage are attracted by the Christian marriages they see. Unbelievers who find Christian morality restrictive are attracted by the good lives of the Christians they know. That is because a gospel life is the good life. It is the good, counter-cultural life that commends God our Saviour to our culture.

Questions for reflection

1. Which "type" of person are you? As you look at your life, how do Paul's words here encourage and challenge you?

2. In which areas do you need to pray for greater self-control? What would self-control look like?

3. How can you be compellingly counter-cultural at home and/or at work this week?

PART TWO

The Context of the Good Life

Titus 2:1-10 outlines the *content* of the good life which the gospel creates. But these verses also describe the *context* in which this good life is to be lived. And that context is a community in which people are discipling one another.

The context for discipleship is not simply, or mainly, going on discipleship courses or reading discipleship books, but everyday life within the Christian family.

Think about the parallel with biological families. Just as children are nurtured in the context of their biological family, so Christians are nurtured in the context of the church family. This may involve courses or programmes or regular one-to-one meetings, just as parents may set aside a regular time for reading the Bible and praying with their children. But parents also nurture their children through a thousand *ad hoc* interactions: we plan outings; we challenge bad behaviour; we involve children when we serve others; we discuss events; we answer their questions; we ask them questions. Good parenting often responds to unplanned situations, but with a high level of **intentionality**. We use the events of our children's lives as opportunities to shape their character and teach the gospel.

It is the same with discipling one another in the church family. We may well want to have organised times when we meet with people to study the Bible and pray together. But we also need to be sharing our lives so that young Christians can see older Christians modelling the good life, and older Christians have opportunities to shape the lives of younger Christians. And the high divorce rates in countries such as the UK and the US make this need even more pressing—we have a generation of young people from dysfunctional homes who need to experience Christian families in action before they themselves become husbands, wives and parents.

This was the context in which Jesus trained his disciples: around a meal, walking along the road or reflecting on events. In the same way, Paul says in 1 Thessalonians 2:8: "Because we loved you so much, we were delighted to share with you not only the gospel of God but our lives as well".

Paul shared the gospel of God in the context of sharing his life with people. As you share your life, and share in others' lives, people will see Christian living modelled, and you will see Christian living modelled to you. Even your failures to live the good life to which we are called become opportunities for learning, if in those situations you model faith in God's grace.

Clearly leaders have an important role to play. After all, Paul is writing this chapter to a church leader. But, according to Ephesians 4:11-12, the role of church leaders is "to equip [God's] people for works of service, so that the body of Christ may be built up". And that is what is going on in Titus 2: Titus is told to disciple people so that they can disciple one another.

So discipleship takes place in community. Christians don't thrive as lone sheep; we are meant to live in flocks. And an important feature of that community-based discipleship is that it happens across generations. The whole letter is about an older man nurturing the faith and ministry of a younger one. Here in Titus **2:3-4**, Paul wants older women to teach what is good and live out what is good, so that they can "urge" or "train" (NIV1984) the younger women. This is cross-generational discipleship.

Respect your Elders

The very term "elders" (1:5) reinforces this. For many of us, "elder" has simply become a jargon word for a church leader. But it means "an older man". This does not mean we should appoint the oldest men in the church as leaders, as it is character, not age, that qualifies a man (1:6-9). Not every older man should be an elder. And being a younger man should not be a bar to eldership; Paul tells Timothy, a leader in a church, not to let anyone look down on him for his youth (1 Timothy 4:12—Timothy was probably in his thirties at this point!). But the fact remains that elders are ordinarily older men. They are people with experience of life and living the faith. There is a proper authority that goes with age.

> There is a proper authority that goes with age.

So in Titus 2, Paul is seeking to paint a picture of a community in which:

- older men and older women are teaching younger men and younger women

- younger people are seeking out the advice of older people

- older people are setting an example to younger people

- younger people are submitting to the direction of older people.

This is a community in which age and experience matter. So key applications of this passage are:

- if you are young, find someone to disciple you

- if you are old, find someone to disciple

- if you consider yourself somewhere in between, then do both!

This, too, is profoundly counter-cultural. Our culture is obsessed both with youth and with personal freedom. In our culture, old people are irrelevant. Aged parents are considered a problem that needs to be solved. Trends are set by the young, and the young define what is important. We choose the new thing over the old thing.

Think about it like this. If you call someone "old" or "old man", you are being negative. It might be a joke, but the joke only works because old is bad in our culture. This is not normal! This is not how it has been in the past. This is not how it is in most of the world. We knew a couple who spent time in the Middle East. The attitude to older people was one of the most striking contrasts they found on their return. In the Middle East, there is complete respect for age. Young people do not even talk when old people are present, unless spoken to. Coming back into western culture, my friends found the way young people treated older people or their parents made them wince. And the Bible urges an attitude far more like the one that couple found in the Middle East than the one they knew back home: "Grey hair is a crown of splendour" (Proverbs 16:31). "Listen to your father, who gave you life, and do not despise your mother when she is old" (Proverbs 23:22).

This attitude to age is counter-cultural in the west. But we already know from Titus 1 that we are to be counter-cultural when the gospel confronts our culture. The God-given context for the good life is a community in which older people are "worthy of respect" (Titus 2:2) and treated with respect, and in which older people teach younger people how to live God's good life.

> We are to be counter-cultural when the gospel confronts our culture.

Our culture has lost the willingness to be fathered or mothered. We should have a desire to be guided and shaped by an older person. This passage encourages us to look for father figures or to look for mothers in the faith.

Perhaps this hardly needs to be said, but notice that discipling is from men to men and largely from women to women. Titus is to "teach the older men" (v 2), "teach the older women" (v 3), "encourage the young men" (v 6) and "teach slaves" (v 9). But **verse 4** says of the older women that, as Titus teaches them to live out the gospel, "then they can urge the younger women...". The one group Titus is not told to teach is the young women—no doubt to avoid temptation or any hint of immorality.

This means that if younger women are to be taught, then older women must be their teachers. It means that older women must take responsibility for discipling the younger women in the church. And it means younger women should seek out older women to guide them in marriage and motherhood and life in general.

How do we Disciple One Another?

You almost certainly don't know John Miller. But I hope you know someone like John Miller—someone who has done and is doing for you what John Miller did for me. And I hope you are, or aspire to be, someone like John Miller yourself.

John led the church plant in London with which my wife and I were involved before we moved to Sheffield. He played a huge role in my development as a leader, as a Christian and indeed as a man. I had only been married three years, and my wife and I had just bought a house. So I went to John for advice on DIY, on cars and on life. One of the first things we did together was replace the guttering on our house.

John and I co-led the church. But he was ten years older than me, and it was clearly a relationship in which he was the senior partner. When we disagreed, I followed his lead, because I trusted his wisdom more than my own. He had a big influence on my preaching, and I learned from him a willingness to try new things and to change what we were doing for the sake of mission.

We were both working full-time in jobs outside the church, so I saw him pouring himself sacrificially into ministry. He used to prepare sermons on the train to and from his job.

More than anything, he taught me how to pray. Prayer for John is not a duty. He prays as if everything depends on God, because he truly believes that it does. I thank God for his influence on my life. He was a Titus 2-type of older man to me when I was young. I hope that I can be that older man to others now. And, whether you're new to church or leading a church or somewhere in between, Titus 2 encourages you to find a John Miller and/or be a John Miller. We all need the other generation far more than we think we do.

This may mean that at some point soon (or right now) you are going to be thinking: *How do I do this? How do I disciple someone? How can I be one of these older women teaching younger women? What does it mean to be a spiritual father to someone?*

Verses 7-8 help. This is how Titus is told to do it: "In everything set them an example by doing what is good. In your teaching show integrity, seriousness and soundness of speech." There are two things here.

1. *Set an example.* Open up your life; have people in your home; take them with you when you do things. Let people see the way you live. Let them see your marriage and your parenting. Of course, you will not always model godly behaviour to them. But, as we have already noted, you then have an opportunity to model the impact of God's grace in our lives.

   This is not just about teaching the Bible. It is also teaching someone to bake a cake, manage a budget, check the car oil, hang a shelf or write a CV. One of the lovely things about the church is that it is a place where we can learn "life skills", both for eternity and for today.

2. *Teach the gospel.* Sometimes this might be more planned as you study through a book of the Bible together or read a Christian book. But often it will be *ad hoc* as you reflect on questions or challenge their behaviour or discuss events.

   Paul describes the characteristics of healthy gospel teaching. We teach people with "integrity" (v 7). In other words, we live what we teach. We teach with "seriousness". In other words, we love what we teach and show that it matters to us. And we teach with "soundness" or "health" (v 8). In other words, teach what will lead to spiritual and emotional health. That means more than telling people how they should live the good life, as Paul does in verses 1-10. It also means telling them why they should live the good life—as Paul is about to do in verses 11-15...

Questions for reflection

1. If you are younger, are you respecting your elders in church? How?

2. If you are older, are you deserving of younger people's respect; and are you using your position intentionally to help those younger than you?

3. How do you need to be discipled, or to disciple someone? How will you actively pursue doing this?

5. GRACE AND GLORY: APPEARING AND POWER

In Titus 2:1-10, Paul has described the content of the good life that Titus is to commend to the church in Crete and the context in which people are to be discipled. Now Paul describes the source of this good life.

He is telling us "the things [we] should teach" (**v 15**). These verses will give us what we need to disciple each other. We are to call each other to the self-control and submission of verses 1-10. But supremely we are to teach each other the grace and glory of God in **verses 11-14**.

Verses 1-10 describe what the good life looks like. They give it content. But if all you ever do is reiterate those commands (to others or to yourself) then they are crushing:

Be self-controlled.

I can't.

Well, try harder.

That is not good news. It is not transformative news. It is condemnation, and there is no condemnation for those who are in Christ Jesus (Romans 8:1). No, the heart of our discipleship is the grace and glory of God.

Grace and Glory

Titus **2:11-14** is all one sentence in the original Greek. We can readily reflect this using the text of the NIV with a slight change to the beginning of **verse 12** (in square brackets):

"For the grace of God has appeared that offers salvation to all people [teaching] us to say 'No' to ungodliness and worldly passions, and to live self-controlled, upright and godly lives in this present age…"

Paul says we live between two "appearings". "The grace of God has appeared" (**v 11**, past tense). "We wait for the blessed hope—the appearing of the glory of our great God and Saviour, Jesus Christ" (**v 13**, future tense). The first appearing was an appearing of the grace of God; the second will be an appearing of the glory of God.

It is clear that when Paul talks about the two appearings, he means the two comings of Jesus and the importance of living between these two events. But the language that Paul uses to describe these events is striking. Paul refers to the appearing of grace and the appearing of glory. What he is saying is that the **incarnation** of Jesus, the death of Jesus and the resurrection of Jesus is an appearing of grace. The whole sequence of events can be summed up as an act of grace. And the return of Jesus can be summed up as an act of glory.

This sense that the return of Jesus is an act of glory is reinforced by a careful reading of the text. At first sight, there is an ambiguity in **verse 13**: "the appearing of the glory of our great God and Saviour, Jesus Christ". Does "our great God and Saviour" refer to two persons (the Father and the Son), or to one? And, if it is one person, is it God the Son or God the Father?

The first option is that the verse refers to two persons—the Father and the Son. With this option the verse reads like this: "the appearing of the glory of [first] our great God [= God the Father] and [second] [our] Saviour, Jesus Christ". In other words, the glory of God the Father and God the Son will appear. But this reading is unlikely. The Greek is literally "the great God and Saviour of us". There is only one definite article ("the"), which applies to both the words "God" and "Saviour". Plus, nowhere else does the New Testament talk about God the Father joining Jesus at the second coming.

The second option is that the verse refers to one person—Jesus. With this option, the verse reads like this: "the appearing of the glory of our great God and Saviour, [who is] Jesus Christ". In other words, Paul is talking about the appearing of one person, and that person is Jesus. So both "God" and "Saviour" refer to Jesus. After all, it is Jesus who will appear at the second coming and Jesus is named immediately after the phrase "great God and Saviour". The problem is that a few verses later Paul repeats the phrase "God our Saviour" and there he uses it to refer to God the Father (3:4).

In fact Paul does not actually say Jesus will appear. It is, of course, true that Jesus will appear in person (as Paul affirms elsewhere and is about to affirm in Titus 3). But what Paul actually says will appear in this verse is "the glory" of God. He clearly has in mind the appearing of Jesus, but he describes this as "the appearing of the glory of our great God". What he then affirms is that the glory of God is Jesus.

So the third option is to be preferred, which is that **2:13** refers to one person, who is God the Father. The glory of the Father will appear at the end of history—and the glory of the Father *is* Jesus Christ. So the sense of the verse is this: "the appearing of the glory of our great God and Saviour [God the Father], [and the glory of God the Father is] Jesus Christ." This matches the reference

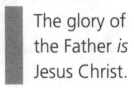

The glory of the Father *is* Jesus Christ.

to God our Saviour a few verses later in 3:4. The characteristics of God (his kindness and love) appear in the person of Jesus. In both **2:13** and 3:4 a characteristic of God (his glory in 2:13 and his kindness in 3:4) appears, and the form in which they each appear is Jesus.

The first coming of Jesus was an act of grace. In the life, death and resurrection of Jesus we see the grace of God the Father. This is precisely the language Paul uses a few verses later in 3:4-5: "But when the kindness and love of God our Saviour appeared, he saved us, not because of righteous things we had done, but because of his mercy". The first coming of Jesus marked the appearing of the grace of God. In a parallel way, the second coming of Jesus will be an act of glory. Through his return, we will see the glory of God the Father. The two great events of history (the first and second comings of Jesus) are revelations respectively of the grace of God and the glory of God.

This pattern of grace and glory matches the way Jesus himself portrayed his coming. The Jews expected a single coming or appearing of God—one event. And when Jesus came there were many features of his ministry that looked like that event. He had authority over sickness, evil and death. But there were also features of his ministry that did not match Jewish expectations. He was despised and rejected. Jesus explained this by saying that his kingdom is going to come in two stages. First, it has come in grace as the offer of salvation. But the parables of the weeds and of the net in Matthew 13 warn us not to misinterpret this. Just because the kingdom has come in grace does not mean that one day it will not come in glory. Grace has appeared; glory will one day appear.

> Grace has appeared; glory will one day appear.

We think of this coming in glory as something that will be wonderful, and indeed it will be for those who belong to Christ. But we need to remember that throughout the Old Testament the glory of God is also seen as a threat. Moses, for example, asks to see God's glory, for it is a wonderful thing. But he can only see the afterglow of the back part of God's glory because otherwise he would be destroyed (Exodus 33). The coming of God's glory is a threat to those who do not know Christ.

The reason that Jesus came first in grace was so that his future coming in glory need not be a threat to his people. His coming in grace culminated in his death on our behalf. And it had to, because we all "fall short of the glory of God, and all are justified freely by his grace through the redemption that came by Christ Jesus [because] God presented [him] as a sacrifice of atonement, through the shedding of his blood—to be received by faith" (Romans 3:23-25).

What is Hidden will Appear

We often talk about "the return of Christ", or "the second coming". But Paul usually uses the word "appearing" (Colossians 3:4; 1 Timothy 6:14; 2 Timothy 4:8). Indeed, the New Testament speaks much more often of Christ's appearing than of his coming. The idea is that Christ now reigns in heaven and he is glorified. That reign and that glory are currently hidden. As you look around the world, you do not see a world under the authority of Jesus. But one day his glory will be revealed. One day every knee will bow before him (Philippians 2:10). What is now true but hidden will one day be revealed for all to see (Revelation 1:7; Job 19:25-27). When Christ comes, we will not see anything that is new. What is different is that we will see it.

And on that day we, too, will appear with him in glory. In Colossians 3:3-4, Paul says: "For you died, and your life is now hidden with Christ in God. When Christ, who is your life, appears, then you also will appear with him in glory." When someone becomes a Christian, the Holy Spirit gives them new life. Indeed without that new life, as we saw when we looked at Titus 1:1-3, you cannot respond to God in faith. Faith is itself a gift given through the regenerating work of the Spirit—life and faith are both given by him, and are given together.

But our resurrection life is not outwardly visible. In fact, as all of us can testify, we are still subject to physical decay. But one day we will have renewed resurrection bodies, and our resurrection life will be both inward and outward. We will appear in glory with Jesus. This is what Paul calls "blessed hope" (2:13)—joyful, happy future certainty.

Does this hope make you happy? It is easy for us to be preoccupied with our present problems or our decaying bodies. So in Colossians

Paul introduces his teaching on our hidden life and Christ's future appearing with this call: "Since, then, you have been raised with Christ, set your hearts on things above, where Christ is, seated at the right hand of God. Set your minds on things above, not on earthly things" (Colossians 3:1-2). By faith we are to lift our eyes from our present problems to heaven, where our glorious future is already a reality.

Between Grace and Glory

Paul's language is striking. He does not talk about the comings of Jesus (though he could have done). He talks about the appearing of grace and the appearing of glory. The source and motives of the good life described in Titus 2:1-10 are the grace and glory of God revealed in Jesus Christ.

The order in which Paul presents this material is also striking:

1. Grace has appeared (v 11)

2. What grace teaches us (v 12)

3. Glory will appear (v 13)

4. How grace teaches us (v 14)

It is worth asking why Paul puts things together in this order. Why not talk about the two appearings, and then talk about what they teach us? Why tell us what grace teaches us and then delay telling us how this process operates?

The answer is that this order mirrors the way we are to live between these two appearings. The order of the text is structured to create a picture of the subject matter it describes. Our behaviour in the text is described between the two appearings because our behaviour in life is lived between these appearings. This is further emphasised by Paul's inclusion of the phrase "in this present age" in **verse 12**. We live with **verse 11** behind us and **verse 13** ahead of us, and we live in light of both. Grace does not simply prepare us for the future age (by saving us from God's judgment). Grace also shapes our lives in the present.

The gospel is good news for the last day. But it is also good news for the next day.

Questions for reflection

1. Think about what is best and what is hardest about your life. How does knowing you live between grace and glory shape your attitude towards those things?

2. Think back to how 2:1-10 challenged you. How will reflecting on the grace and glory of God motivate you to change?

3. Who could you encourage to enjoy God's grace and coming glory today?

PART TWO

The Engine of a Good Life

That we live between the appearing of grace and the appearing of glory is wonderfully encouraging. But we should not miss the reason why Paul describes these two comings. Grace and glory are the engine that drives the good life of verses 1-10. Paul reminds Titus of these two appearings so that Titus can teach these things (**v 15**). These are the truths that Titus must use to "encourage and rebuke" people as he exhorts them to live good lives".

> Grace does not mean that what we do does not matter.

We should not misunderstand Paul's emphasis on grace. Grace does not mean that what we do does not matter. It does not mean that we can live how we choose since God will always forgive us. Paul is quite clear: we need to say "No" to ungodliness and worldly passions. We are to be self-controlled. The three positive virtues refer to all our relationships:

- with ourselves ("self-controlled")

- with others ("upright")

- with God ("godly")

Grace teaches us to control ourselves and our passions. It teaches us to treat other people in an "upright" or "just" manner. And it teaches us to be "godly"—that is, to relate to God rightly.

But what enables and energises this life is God's grace. God's grace is our teacher. There will be times when you need to tell people what a good life looks like. That is what verses 1-10 are for. But if you want people actually to live a good life, then do not emphasise the good they must do for God. Instead, emphasise the good God has done for them. We can summarise how this works by highlighting three things from **verses 13-14**.

New Hope

First, we live the good life. But we await an even better life. "*We wait* for the blessed hope—the appearing of the glory of our great God and Saviour, Jesus Christ" (**v 13**). We look back to the appearing of grace. But, as verse 13 highlights, we also look forward to the appearing of glory. There is, if you like, both a push and a pull in Christian living. We are pushed from behind by the wonder of grace and we are pulled forward by the hope of glory.

This is why Paul's language is so significant. As we have seen, he does not refer simply to the return of Christ. He refers to the appearing of glory. Our blessed hope is the hope of glory. The attractions of this world do not gleam so brightly when compared to the treasures of the world to come. The pleasures of sin do not attract so strongly when compared to the joy of the world to come. Our model is Moses. "He chose to be ill-treated along with the people of God rather than to enjoy the fleeting pleasures of sin" (Hebrews 11:25). Why? Because "he regarded disgrace for the sake of Christ as of greater value than the treasures of Egypt, because he was looking ahead to his reward" (v 26).

This "glory" is not some undefined or unspecified reward. That is why we took the time to understand Titus **2:13**. Our blessed hope is the appearing of the glory of God, and the glory of God is Jesus Christ. Our hope is a person. In **verse 12**, Paul says we are to "say 'No' to ungodliness". The word ungodliness (*asebeia*) is used in Romans 1:18, where it introduces Paul's description of the way humanity has exchanged the glory of God for idols. But grace teaches us that the Creator is better, fuller and richer than anything that has been created and that we could worship as an idol. The prospect of glory is the prospect of seeing and enjoying the glory of the God who is better, fuller and richer. Choosing God instead of the immediate and visible pleasures of sin can be tough. It is an act of faith. But faith recognises that ultimately God in Christ is always better, fuller and richer. And glory will be the fulfilment, realisation and culmination of that present faith.

New Love

Second, we await a Saviour "who gave himself for us" (**v 14**). Jesus gave himself for me and this love wins my heart. "The life I now live in the body," says Paul in Galatians 2:20, "I live by faith in the Son of God, who loved me and gave himself for me".

Why do I serve my wife? Not because I must. I do not have to win her love. She has already given herself to me. I serve my wife because I love her, and my love for her is fed by her love for me.

Why do I serve my Saviour? Not because I must. I do not have to win his love. He has already given himself for me. I serve my Saviour because I love him, and my love for him is fed by his love for me. "We love because he first loved us" (1 John 4:19).

New Identity

We await a Saviour "who gave himself for us to redeem us from all wickedness and to purify for himself a people that are his very own, eager to do what is good" (Titus **2:14**). Who are we? We are God's people, God's very own people, purified for good works. Who are you? You are God's child, his own child, purified by the blood of his Son for good works, made pure to be pure, set apart for a good life. Paul is picking up the language of the exodus and the promise of a new exodus (see Psalm 130:8; Ezekiel 37:23). Jesus gave himself to "redeem us" (Titus 2:14). It is the language of releasing slaves. "A people for his own possession" (**v 14**, ESV) echoes Exodus 19:5: "You will be my treasured possession". We live holy lives because we are God's treasured possession, bought with the blood of his own Son, liberated from the slavery of sin to live a new life that displays God's goodness to the world.

Legalism says: *What we do leads to who we are.* Legalism says, for example, that if we live a righteous life, then we can become righteous people. But the gospel rejects this. The gospel declares that being righteous is God's gift to us. This is the grace of God.

Who we are is graciously given to us by God the Father through the redemptive work of God the Son and the renewing work of the Holy Spirit.

But grace does not say: *What we do does not matter.* That is the cry of what is known as **antinomianism**. No, the true corrective to legalism's claim that what we do leads to who we are is to turn this on its head. Grace says: *Who we are leads to what we do.* That is what Paul is saying here. Christ has made: "a people that are his very own". Nothing we do can make us or unmake us as Christ's people. But those who are Christ's people will be "eager to do what is good". We do not do good so that we can become Christ's people. Christ makes his people so that we become eager to do good.

There is a story told of the late Queen Mother of the British royal family. When her children, Princess Elizabeth (now Queen Elizabeth II) and Princess Margaret, were young and were going to a party or on a visit, she would remind them before they left: "Royal children have royal manners". It was a reminder that their behaviour needed to match their status. Their status came first; their behaviour should follow. These verses are teaching the same thing to Christians. He has made us part of his people. In Christ, we are members of the royal family of the universe. That is our status, and we cannot lose it. And our behaviour should match who we are. Royal children have royal manners.

> In Christ, we are members of the royal family of the universe.

That is why, Paul says, Jesus "gave himself for us": to make us royal children who would live with royal manners. Or, as he puts it, Christ gave himself for us:

- To redeem us from all wickedness

- To purify for himself a people that are his very own

These two reasons in Titus **2:14** correspond to the negatives and positives of **verse 12**:

■ "To redeem us from all wickedness" corresponds to: "It teaches us to say 'No' to ungodliness and worldly passions"

■ "To purify for himself a people that are his very own" corresponds to: "It teaches us ... to live self-controlled, upright and godly lives"

So, why do we say *No* to ungodliness? Because Jesus has redeemed us from ungodliness. Why do we say *Yes* to godliness? Because Jesus has purified us and because we belong to him.

The engine of a good life is our new hope, our new love and our new identity from God our Saviour. "These, then, are the things you should teach" (**v 15**). These things are to form the content of Titus' encouragement and rebukes. But then, rather strangely, Paul adds: "Do not let anyone despise you". What does it mean, to encourage with the gospel and rebuke in the gospel in a way that prevents anyone despising you? It might mean that Titus is not to bow to pressure to water down the gospel by reducing its demands, or to add to the gospel like the circumcision group. Titus is to stick to teaching the gospel without being bullied by other people's attitudes. Or it could mean that Titus is to live what he preaches, so as to give no cause for people to despise him for hypocrisy (as Paul has said in 2:7). Perhaps it is a bit of both. Titus is both to talk the talk and walk the walk without wavering from the gospel of grace.

The Engine of a Missional Life

Verses 11-14 not only provide the basis for the good life described throughout verses 1-10. **Verse 11** also picks up the concern for the **missional** implications of our behaviour that has run through Paul's exhortations in this chapter:

■ "so that no one will malign the word of God" (v 5)

- "so that those who oppose you may be ashamed because they have nothing bad to say about us" (v 8)

- "so that in every way they will make the teaching about God our Saviour attractive" (v 10)

Notice the repeated use of the phrase "so that". We are to behave in a way that is appropriate to sound doctrine so that no one will malign the gospel, and so that the gospel will be attractive to people.

Verse 11 provides the rationale for this behaviour. Why should we make the teaching about God our Saviour attractive? Because, according to verse 11, the salvation of God comes to all people. The ESV translates this verse as: "For the grace of God has appeared, bringing salvation for all people". The NIV 2011 softens this assertion by translating it as: "For the grace of God has appeared that offers salvation to all people." But literally, Paul says: "The grace of God appeared saving all men".

Does this mean Paul is a universalist? Does he mean every individual will be saved? We know enough of the New Testament to realise that this understanding of the verse is unlikely. Paul and the other New Testament writers are clear that many people will be condemned on the final day of judgment (see, for instance, 2 Thessalonians 1:6-10). It is important to read this verse in its context. Paul has just been addressing different groups of people within the church. He ends by addressing slaves. Now he says that grace brings salvation to all people. What he means is all the classes of people about whom he has just been talking. Grace brings salvation to men and women, young and old, slave and free.

This is important, because Titus **2:11** begins: "For...". This is the reason why we should adopt the behaviour described in verses 1-10. Why should older men be temperate? So they commend the gospel to other older men, because Christ came to save old people. Why should older women be reverent? So they commend the gospel to other women, because Christ came to save women. Why should younger women love their husbands and children? So they commend the gospel to them, because Christ came to husbands and children. Why should young men be self-controlled? So they commend the gospel to other younger men, because Christ came to save young men. Why should slaves be subject to their masters? So they commend the gospel to their masters, because Christ came to save masters. We could go on.

Cretan culture was characterised by drunkenness and promiscuity—much like many cities today. Paul's message clearly involved turning away from that way of life. But it was not a message of abstinence. He was not trying to persuade people to give up a life of fun for a life without fun. He was offering people a life of salvation, a life that is more satisfying.

It is important to recognise Paul's logic here. Paul is not to trying to persuade Christians to see their life as attractive, in the sense of being easy. Instead, he expects that unbelievers will be attracted to this new life in Christ. Paul is saying that unbelievers will find life in Christ compelling, even though that life is often counter-cultural and frequently costly. People will look at our lives and say: *I want to live like that* or: *I want to grow old like that*. And if they are attracted to our lives, then they may start to show an interest in our message.

> If people are attracted to our lives, they may start to show an interest in our message.

God does not save all people, but he does save all kinds of people—so we all need to live in a way that commends the gospel to all kinds of people. It is only as we live the gospel and preach the gospel that it becomes clear who God's elect are, as they respond with Spirit-given faith. We see this working in practice in Pisidian Antioch in Acts 13. We are told that "almost the whole city" of Pisidian Antioch gathered to hear Paul and Barnabas preach (Acts 13:44). Afterwards we are told: "When the Gentiles heard this, they were glad and honoured the word of the Lord; and all who were appointed for eternal life believed" (verse 48). Paul preached to all the city—and those who were chosen by God responded with faith.

Questions for reflection

1. In what way will you say "no" to ungodliness today? How will the gospel be the engine of that?

2. Which temptations don't gleam so bright to you when you set them alongside the glory you are heading for?

3. New hope… new love… new identity. Which of these is particularly precious to you today?

6. KINDNESS AND RENEWAL

I wonder how you think of God.

Maybe he feels distant to you. Maybe he seems a little harsh or high-handed. Or maybe you feel that he has forgiven you, so now he tolerates you.

If "kind" is not a word we quickly think of, then we need to meet and be thrilled by the God Paul speaks of here: "When the kindness and love of God our Saviour appeared..." (3:4).

Paul will finish this section (verses 4-7 are a single sentence in Greek) with the words: "This is a trustworthy saying" (**v 8a**). This way of referring to what he's just said suggests that verses 4-7 may have been an existing hymn or creed which Paul is quoting before adding his own affirmation. We are meant to read it, reflect on it, trust it and marvel at the God it reveals to us—a God whose kindness and love have appeared.

Facing the Truth about Ourselves

This description of God's kindness is prefaced with these words: "At one time we too were foolish, disobedient, deceived and enslaved by all kinds of passions and pleasures. We lived in malice and envy, being hated and hating one another" (**v 3**).

Our relationship with God was a mess. We were "foolish" and "disobedient". In the Bible, a fool is someone who "says in his heart,

---

* Verses 1-2 are covered in the following chapter.

'There is no God'" (Psalm 14:1). A fool is not necessarily an avowed atheist; it is someone who lives as if God does not exist. To ignore God is the definition of folly. And a disobedient person is someone who rejects God's rule and wants to run their own life. This rejection of God then affects everything else:

- our thinking—we were foolish and deceived

- our behaviour—we were disobedient and enslaved

It is also something for which we are responsible and at the same time we are victims:

- we are responsible—we were foolish and disobedient

- we are victims—we were deceived and enslaved

How does this work? Our individual choices have created a collective culture that deceives us. The world pushes us into its mould, but it is a world we have created together. And our choices have created patterns of personal behaviour that enslave us. We are trapped by our habits, but they are habits we formed through our actions. As a result, we are helpless. We need someone to save us. Often people will admit they are not perfect and need some help. But we need more than a helping hand. We need a complete rescue.

Because our relationship with God is a mess, our relationships with one another are a mess. In foolish disobedience, we have: "lived in malice and envy, being hated and hating one another" (**Titus 3:3**). Malice is wishing bad things would happen to people; envy is wishing good things had not happened to people.

You may be thinking: *I thought we were going to talk about kindness and love, and here we are talking about malice and hatred!* Imagine someone saying to you: *I think you're stupid, selfish, gullible and everyone hates you.* You would hardly respond: *It's very kind of you to say so!*

Twenty-first-century western culture is all about self-esteem and self-image. It is all about me and how I feel about myself. So if anyone threatens that with an uncompromising dose of truth, then it feels like an attack on me. We must all pretend we are wonderful people, and ignore and excuse all evidence to the contrary. But because of the good news of Jesus, there is no need for pretending. This constant, tiring attempt to manage our image, to portray ourselves in the best light, can all be over.

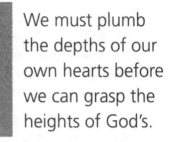

> We must plumb the depths of our own hearts before we can grasp the heights of God's.

The reality is that we will never understand the wonderful kindness and love of God until we face the reality of what we are like without him. We are hated and we are hating. We must read **verse 3** with **verse 4**. We must plumb the depths of our own hearts before we can grasp the heights of God's.

Enjoying the Truth about God's Kindness

"He saved" (**v 5**) is the main verb of the sentence that runs from verse 4 to verse 7 in the Greek. We were facing condemnation, judgment and death. And there was nothing we could do. We were deceived and enslaved. We were powerless and helpless. But he saved.

Do you ever make decisions by drawing up a list of pros and cons? Imagine God deciding whether to save us with a list of pros and cons. What is on the "cons" side—what are the reasons why God should condemn us? *Foolish, disobedient, deceived, enslaved, malicious, envious, hated, hating.* And what is on the "pros" side? What is in the list of reasons why God should save us? *Nothing.* There is no reason why God should save us. But then God writes across the page: *My kindness. My love. My mercy.*

God did not look at us and think: *On balance, they're not too bad.* He did not look at us and think: *I can see some potential there.* He saw folly, disobedience, malice, envy and hatred. He saw a thousand reasons to condemn us for ever.

And yet in his kindness and love, he saved us: "not because of righteous things we had done, but because of his mercy" (**v 5**). God writes across the pages of your future: *My kindness. My love. My mercy.*

"He saved us ... because". The word "because" is key. Here is the reason for our acceptance by God, the grounds of our confidence and the basis of our hope. It is worth asking ourselves: *How would I complete the sentence, "He accepts me because..."?*

Everyone answers that question somehow. If I think I will be saved because of something I have done, then I am not saved. I can have no confidence. Our acceptance before God is: "Not because of righteous things we [have] done" (**v 5**). Saving faith involves re-moving faith in ourselves. It involves stripping away confidence in anything except God. "He saved us ... because of his mercy". That is our true and only hope.

And if you think that I will be accepted because you are inherently acceptable, or because God should accept everyone regardless, then I am not saved. We should have no confidence. We need to re-read **verse 3** and feel the weight of the truth about who we are and what we are like, and see that God's kindness does not mean injustice. He will punish sin.

Our salvation begins with the mercy of God the Father. This is fundamentally important. It is not that Jesus had to persuade God the Father to save us. It is not that Jesus is the nice guy who had to intervene to stop an angry God hating us. It all begins with the kindness and love of God the Father.

The Grace of God the Son

And there was a point in time "when the kindness and love of God our Saviour appeared, [and] he saved us" (**v 4-5**). The kindness and love of God have been there all along, intrinsic to who he is—but there was a moment when they appeared in history. And that moment was the first Christmas day.

Jesus is the kindness and love of God made visible. Humanity had heard about the love of God over the centuries, as it were, in the promises of God and through the prophets. But at the first Christmas, God's kindness became more than a rumour, more than a promise. It became physical. People could see it and touch it. God has always loved us, but in the incarnation and, most of all, at the crucifixion, his love reached a climax as he gave what was most precious to him, his own Son, to live as a human and die as a criminal. Just how great is the kindness and love of God? Look at the crib; look at the cross. Look at God giving his own beloved Son.

> At the first Christmas, God's kindness became more than a rumour.

As Paul goes on, he has the work of both God the Spirit and God the Son, according to the plan of God the Father, in view. We'll focus first on the work of the Son.

When we chose to ignore and disobey God, we became God's enemies. We became rebels under his judgment, and so our future was condemnation and death. And before there could be reconciliation, God had to deal with that disobedience. The penalty of our rebellion had to be paid. The sentence of death had to be passed. So in his kindness and love, God the Father sent his Son to die in our place.

And as a result, first, we have been "justified" (**v 7**). Justified is a legal term, meaning to be declared right. A trial is taking place. The charge is that we are foolish, disobedient, deceived, enslaved, malicious, envious, hated and hating. There is more than enough evidence against us and the verdict must surely be *Guilty*. But then the kindness of God intervenes. It appears in the form of his Son. The sentence we deserve is passed on him. He dies in our place and bears our penalty.

As a result, the verdict against us is no longer one of condemnation, but innocence. We are justified.

Second, as a result, we receive life. We were justified so that "we might become heirs having the hope of eternal life" (**v 7**). Paul is repeating what he said at the beginning of the letter, where he described salvation in the same way—"the hope of eternal life" (1:2).

So in **3:7**, Paul is linking justification with the hope of eternal life. The verse begins "so that". Eternal life is the consequence of the work of the Spirit described in **verse 5**. The Spirit opens our eyes to recognise Jesus as our Saviour so that we put our faith in him. And it is by this Spirit-given faith in the finished work of Jesus that we are justified. But that is not all. Paul presents justification as a precondition of having hope. It is only "having been justified by his grace" that we can "become heirs having the hope of eternal life" (**v 7**).

Justification is therefore present-focused and forward-looking. We are justified in the present through the resurrection of Jesus. Through his resurrection, Jesus was vindicated—it was the affirmation that the death of Jesus truly was an effective sacrifice for sin. It was, and is, the Father's great "Yes" to the Son. The Lord Jesus is justified—and we are justified in him. As a result, we experience peace with God, because God treats us as he treats his Son.

> God treats us as he treats his Son.

And so we are "heirs" (**v 7**). Heirs are children with the rights of inheritance. I have sometimes been given a meal or place to stay by someone because I was a friend of their son. They welcomed me for the sake of their son. It was only my relationship with him that meant I sat at their table, enjoyed their company, and slept in their home. How much more does God delight to welcome us for the sake of his Son! Our standing before God has changed right here and right now.

Yet the trial has not yet taken place. We are still waiting for the final day of judgment. Our justification now is an anticipation of that day.

It is the anticipation of the "not guilty" verdict which we will certainly hear on the final day.

But our hope is not simply the promise of acquittal on the day of judgment. That day is, as we shall see when we look at verse 5 in Part Two, also the day when God renews all things. So our hope is "the hope of eternal life" (v 7). The phrase "eternal life" is literally "life of the coming age". Our hope is the certainty that we will live a new life in a renewed world. The kindness of God has not only saved us from something, but for something. Left to ourselves, our future was eternal death. In Christ, it is now eternal life.

Questions for reflection

1. How has reflecting on these verses changed the way you think and feel about God today?

2. Take some time to reflect on your own innate sinfulness, and to confess it to God. How does knowing more of who you are affect your appreciation of what God the Son came to do for you?

3. How would you explain God's kindness to someone who is not a Christian?

PART TWO

Father, Spirit and Son

The "trustworthy saying" (**v 8a**) of verses 4-7 begins with the mercy of God the Father, and ends with the grace of God the Son. But at its centre is the renewal of God the Spirit, and it's to this that we now turn.

The normal order in which we talk about the Trinity is Father, Son and Holy Spirit. That is the order in which the persons of the Trinity work in history. The Father sends the Son, and then together they send the Holy Spirit. At the **instigation** of the Father, the Son entered human history at the incarnation, and then the Spirit entered human history at **Pentecost**. This was the order Jesus himself employed when he commanded us to make disciples and baptise them "in the name of the Father and of the Son and of the Holy Spirit" (Matthew 28:19).

But here, Paul presents the work of God in a different order. He starts with the Father's mercy in Titus **3:4-5**. This, he says, has "appeared"—and we know God's mercy appeared in Jesus (2:11). But Paul does not mention Jesus by name at this point. Instead, he moves on to describe the work of the Spirit in **3:5**, and only then does he describe the work of Jesus in **verses 6-7**. What does this switch of order signify?

Father, Son, Spirit is the order we see in history. But Father, Spirit, Son is the order we see in our personal experience. Jesus has appeared in history, but left to ourselves we do not recognise his grace. So our experience of God begins with the Father's merciful initiative. In his mercy he sends the Spirit to open our blind eyes and renew our dead hearts so that we recognise Jesus. Only then do we see the death of Jesus as God's victory and the shame of the cross as God's glory.

The Renewal of God the Spirit

When we looked at **verse 7**, we saw that Jesus got what we deserve. He endured our condemnation and death. In return, we get what Jesus deserves: we get his reward.

And what is the reward that Jesus deserves and that we get, poured out generously? It is God himself, in the person of the Spirit. It is God's fatherly presence in our hearts. The Father "saved us through the washing of rebirth and renewal by the Holy Spirit, whom he poured out on us generously through Jesus Christ our Saviour" (**v 5-6**).

God measures out the Spirit to us in accordance with what his Son deserves. How much do you think that is? How much do you think Jesus is worth to God? The Spirit has been poured out "generously". This is not like pouring out a cup of water. This is like standing under a waterfall with a constant rush flowing over us.

How much do you expect of the Spirit's work in your life? The answer depends on what you think the death of Jesus is worth to God. This is the Son's reward: the Father pouring out the Spirit on his people, giving us rebirth and renewal.

> The Spirit has been poured out like a waterfall, with a constant rush flowing over us.

"Rebirth" (**v 5**) is often translated "regeneration". It is a term with which we are familiar. We talk about urban, economic or neighbourhood regeneration. And these terms mean improvement in some form; perhaps even a huge transformation. But biblical regeneration is very different. It involves so much more than mere improvement. "Rebirth" captures what it involves much better. We are dead—and then we are reborn. It is not that we are living badly, and then, after a regeneration programme, we look better and live better. No, we are dead in our sin, and then we are reborn. We begin a new life.

The word "renewal" describes the same radical transformation. Again, we often used the word "renewal" to mean "repeat". If you renew a subscription, for example, then you are simply continuing to receive what you are already receiving. But this renewal is not merely new in time, but new in nature.

Remember, we were "deceived" and "enslaved" (v 3). We could not turn to God, because we were in chains. And we did not even want to turn to him, because we were deceived. So when the love and kindness of God appeared in Jesus—when Jesus died to save all who put their faith in him, opening the door to eternal life—it made absolutely no difference to us. Left to ourselves none of us would ever enter because we are deceived and enslaved. There is God, loving us, dying for us, welcoming us; and all we feel is malice and envy and hatred. There is no salvation without rebirth and renewal. Unless we become new people with new hearts and new desires and new loves, then we will never turn back to God. Unless the Spirit works in us, we will not want eternal life with God, and we will not see that the door to it is open, and we will not walk through it.

> Unless the Spirit works in us, we will not want eternal life with God.

This is why the language of rebirth and renewal is so significant. A baby cannot decide to be born, and neither can a person decide to be born again. It is only God the Spirit, at the merciful initiative of God the Father, who gives new life. In God's kindness and love "he saved us through the washing of rebirth and renewal by the Holy Spirit" (**v 5**).

Commentators divide on whether Paul is talking about baptism when he speaks about "the washing of rebirth". I think it must be an allusion to baptism, because water baptism was so significant in the life of the church. Paul's readers would naturally have assumed he was talking about baptism. But what is important to say is that baptism is not the moment when regeneration takes place. It is not that I decide to follow Christ by being baptised, and therefore as a result I am born again. It is the other way round: I am reborn by the Spirit at God's initiative, and therefore as a result I decide to follow Jesus. Baptism is the great celebration and reminder of God's initiative in regeneration.

This is what is going on when someone becomes a Christian. It might be that someone says: *I've read the Bible and I've decided that it's true so I'm going to believe in Jesus.* Or someone might say: *I've seen the lives of Christians and I've heard the message so I've decided to follow Jesus for myself.* Or someone might say: *I love God because of all that he's done for me so I've decided to be baptised.* Maybe you can hear yourself in one of those descriptions of someone becoming a Christian. And that is great. All those descriptions are true. That is what happens from our personal, human perspective.

But in every case there is something going on beforehand and underneath. And that is the Spirit's work of rebirth. If you have decided that the Bible is true, it is because the Spirit has opened your eyes to see Jesus. If you have decided to follow Jesus, it is because the Spirit has opened your heart to love Jesus.

Do you see what God is doing? In his kindness and his love he has provided for every step of the way. He does not say: *I've done all this for you. Now the rest is up to you.* No—he provides every single thing we need. He even provides the recognition that we need him for everything! That is how kind he is. This is how the hymn-writer John Stocker responded in 1776:

Thy mercy, my God, is the theme of my song,

the joy of my heart and the boast of my tongue.

Thy free grace alone, from the first to the last,

hath won my affections and bound my soul fast.

Cosmic, as well as Personal

And the kindness and love of God is even greater than what we have seen! The New Testament talks a lot about "new birth" or "rebirth". But the word Paul uses here in **verse 5** when he talks about "the washing of rebirth" is only used on one other occasion. It literally means "new beginning". The other time it is used is in Matthew 19:28, when Jesus says: "Truly I tell you, at the renewal of all things, when the Son of Man sits on his glorious throne, you who have followed me will also sit on twelve thrones, judging the twelve tribes of Israel."

Jesus here is not talking about a person becoming a Christian. He is talking about the renewal, or the rebirth, or the new beginning, of all things. He is not talking about the renewal of one life, but the renewal of all life. The focus is cosmic, not personal: a new world, a new universe, a new creation. Paul uses the same birth metaphor in Romans 8:22: "We know that the whole creation has been groaning as in the pains of childbirth right up to the present time". At the moment, with disasters and sickness and death, creation is feeling labour pains. But labour pains are signs that soon there will be a birth! Soon the whole creation will experience a "rebirth", a new beginning.

So how does this fit with Paul's use of the word here in Titus? What does the conversion of me, Tim Chester, forty years ago have to do with the renewal of all things at the end of time?

The answer is that when you become a Christian, you are being made ready for a new creation. Imagine God were to make a beautiful new world and then fill it with people who are "foolish, disobedient, deceived and enslaved … [living] in malice and envy, being hated and hating one another" (Titus **3:3**). It would be a disaster; we would ruin it all over again. So first he gives us rebirth and renewal through the Holy Spirit. In fact, God only delays the renewal of all things while he patiently gets his people ready (Romans 2:4). If we are to be part of the world reborn, then we ourselves need to be reborn. Paul says here in Titus **3:7** that God saved us so that "we might become heirs having the hope of eternal life."

> What God is doing in your heart is the first glimpse of the new creation.

And this means that your rebirth and renewal by the Holy Spirit is part of God's work of rebirthing and renewing all things. What God is doing in your heart is the first glimpse of the new creation.

It is worth dwelling on this truth for a moment. Think about your local church or your house group. Imagine them gathered together, and then look round the room in your imagination. God's new world—so radically different from our own—has begun among these people. God's new world has begun in your heart. Through his Spirit, God is already living in you. Through his Spirit, God is already renewing you, giving you a heart of love and purity and joy, a life that reflects his glory. As James says: "He chose to give us birth through the word of truth, that we might be a kind of firstfruits of all he created" (James 1:18). Or as Paul puts it in his letter to the Romans: "The creation itself will be liberated from its bondage to decay and brought into the freedom and glory of the children of God" (Romans 8:21).

Measuring the Kindness of God

How great is the kindness and love of God? Let's finish by trying to measure it!

1. *There is nothing more that he could have given.* He has given us himself. He has kindly and lovingly given us his Son (Titus **3:4**). And he has generously poured out on us his Spirit (**v 6**).

2. *There is nothing more that he could have done.* He has done everything. He has justified us, with no cost to us and at great cost to himself (**v 7**). He has given us new birth; he has renewed us (**v 5**). Every step of the way, he has provided for us. Everything that was needed and is needed, he has done and is doing.

3. *There is nothing more that he could have promised.* He has promised us eternal life in a world reborn (1:2-3; **3:5-7**). He saved us to become heirs, looking forward with certain hope to an eternity spent enjoying everything that Christ deserves (**v 7**). This is "the hope of eternal life", and it is promised by God, "who does not lie" (1:2).

And to whom does he do all this? Those who were foolish, disobedient, deceived, enslaved, living in malice and envy, hating and hated. It is nothing to do with our righteousness, since we have none. It is all to do with his mercy, which is unfathomable (**3:4-5**).

How are we to respond to the amazing kindness of God? That is the subject of the rest of Titus 3. But for now, we can identify four responses:

- Confidence: our salvation rests on what God has done, not on what we do.

- Humility: we have contributed nothing to our salvation.

- Praise: we thank the Father, Son and Spirit for all they have done for us.

- Love: we love God for his kindness to us.

How do you think of God? Kindness and love—rebirth and renewal. That's the God of Father, Spirit and Son—and we can live today, and will live eternally, to praise him.

Questions for reflection

1. *Thy mercy, my God, is the theme of my song.* How will you make sure this is true of you today, and tomorrow?

2. God has poured out his Spirit on you as much as Jesus deserves to have that Spirit poured out on him. How does this change your view of your life, and of your Father?

3. Reflect on the four responses to God's kindness on page 101-102. Which do you find comes least naturally? How will meditating on God's kindness increase that response in you?

7. STRESS THESE THINGS, LIVE THESE THINGS

Verses 3-7 are a beautiful summary of the kindness of God to people who do not deserve it. God's kindness is seen in the sending of his Son and the sending of his Spirit, so that we might share in the rebirth of all things.

But that wonderful sentence is set in the context of Titus 3 as a whole. Paul sets out these verses, perhaps quoting an early hymn or creed, for a purpose. So the question is: what are we to "do" with this wonderful gospel summary?

Stress These Things

Some things are "excellent and profitable" (**v 8**); others are "unprofit-able and useless" (**v 9**). Part of growing in the Christian life is learning which is which.

So what is it that is profitable and excellent? "*This* is a trustworthy saying ... I want you to stress *these things* ... *These things* are excel-lent and profitable for everyone" (**v 8**). "This" and "these things" are references to what Paul has just been talking about in verses 4-7: the kindness of God, the appearing of Jesus, the rebirth of the Spirit, jus-tification by grace, and the hope of eternal life. It is the gospel which is excellent and profitable for everyone: the Father's mercy on us, the Son's work for us, and the Spirit's presence in us.

What are we to do with this? In **verse 8** Paul says: "Stress these things". We are to stress the gospel. We can never talk about the gospel too much. We need never move on from it or move away from it. Stressing these gospel things to our own hearts and to our church family is what we and they most need.

What is unprofitable and useless? "Foolish controversies and genealogies and arguments and quarrels about the law" (**v 9**). And Paul tells Titus to "avoid" these. Stress and avoid—these are the two guidelines of **verses 8-9**. Stress the gospel and avoid controversies. We stress the gospel because it is excellent and profitable, and we avoid controversies because they are unprofitable and useless.

You would not think that was a difficult or contentious thing to say. But the reality is that all too often in church life, we stress controversy and avoid talking about the gospel. It may be true that our preaching stresses the gospel. But our conversations so often stress controversy. The letters and emails that people write stress controversy. The points that people raise stress controversy. We agree on the kindness of the Father, the renewal of the Spirit, the grace of the Son and the hope of eternal life.

> Our preaching stresses the gospel, but our conversations often stress controversy.

And these things are excellent and profitable. But we put our energy into controversies, arguments and quarrels. We do this even though Paul says such things are unprofitable and useless. In other words, they are a waste of time and energy.

What do you discuss at your church business meetings? Do you plan how you will tell the world about the kindness of God, or do you get bogged down in quarrels about things that are unprofitable? When you eat together, hang out together or meet up during the week, what do you talk about? If you go to a Christian conference, what do you talk about in the breaks? Do you talk about the kindness of God, or the latest controversy in the Christian world? Do you prefer reading a blog about some contentious issue, or one that stresses the gospel?

What would Paul say to us? That in every place and every time and with everyone, we should "stress these things"—gospel things. We should talk about the love of the Father, the grace of the Son and the renewal of the Spirit more than we talk about anything else, and we should avoid talking about things that divide, simply because they divide.

The writer to the Hebrews puts it this way: "See to it, brothers and sisters, that none of you has a sinful, unbelieving heart that turns away from the living God. But encourage one another daily, as long as it is called 'Today', so that none of you may be hardened by sin's deceitfulness" (Hebrews 3:12-13). We are all just a few small steps away from being hardened by sin's deceitfulness. Our hearts are extremely good at justifying our sinful desires. And so we need daily encouragement not to turn away from the living God. We need to be a community that is "speaking the [gospel] truth in [gospel] love" to one another in the context of everyday life (Ephesians 4:15).

Warn Divisive People

Next, Paul raises the stakes. He moves from a call to "stress" in Titus **3:8**, to a call to "avoid" in **verse 9**, and then in **verses 10-11** a call to "warn".

In our individualistic culture, we value the individual above the community. So self-expression is one of our highest values. Everyone has a right to express their own opinion, we tell ourselves. But Christ died so that we might be one. He died to reconcile us to God and to reconcile us to one another. In Ephesians 1 Paul says that the climax of God's eternal plan, the fulfilment of his will and his good pleasure, is "to bring unity to all things in heaven and on earth under Christ" (1:10). In Ephesians 2, he describes how the cross has united a divided humanity into one new humanity. In Ephesians 3, he says that it is God's intent that, through the blood-bought unity of the church, "the

manifold wisdom of God should be made known to the rulers and authorities in the heavenly realms" (3:10).

So no wonder that when Paul gets to chapter 4, his exhortation is: "Make every effort to keep the unity of the Spirit through the bond of peace" (4:3). He goes on to talk about not letting the devil get a foothold by letting anger remain unresolved (4:26-27). He says we should only say what will build others up (4:29). He exhorts us to put away bitterness, anger and slander, and replace them with kindness, compassion and forgiveness (4:31-32).

Paul is passionate about unity in the church because this is God's eternal plan—this is why Christ died, and through our unity we display God's wisdom. When viewed in this way, suddenly we can see why there is a need to deal decisively with a divisive person who promotes disunity. This is what is at stake: the purposes of God, the work of the cross and the success of mission.

Here in Titus **3:10**, Paul describes a three-stage process for dealing with someone who is divisive:

1. a first warning,

2. a second warning, and finally

3. **excommunication**.

It corresponds to the process outlined by Jesus in Matthew 18:15-17. Jesus says that if a brother or sister sins, you should point out their fault one to one. If they refuse to listen, then go to them again with someone else. Finally, if they still refuse to listen, you should bring it to the church with a view to the church treating them "as you would a pagan or a tax collector".

People who pick an argument and refuse to **repent** are "warped and sinful" (Titus **3:11**). Their priorities have shifted away from the gospel, so that their conduct is pulled out of shape and warped. "They are self-condemned," says Paul. Their tendency to pick a quarrel reveals their sinful hearts. Their love of controversy reveals that in their hearts is either malice—their intent is to undermine and destroy the church; or pride—they assume they know best and they have appointed themselves as the guardians of truth.

Sometimes, we can think this is a hard balance to strike. We do not want unthinking obedience to church leaders—that is a recipe for immaturity or even abuse. But we do want submission. We need to be church members who "obey [our] leaders and submit to their authority" (Hebrews 13:17, NIV1984). So how do we pursue unifying submission without encouraging or excusing overbearing leadership?

Actually, Titus 3 makes it fairly straightforward. If our elders deny the gospel in any way, then we should challenge them. If they get "these things" wrong, then confront them. But on all other matters trust them. They are the leaders God has given you. Of course, leaders are fallible. They will not always get it right. But do not assume you would do a better job.

I see many people whose default position is to be suspicious of their church leaders. Some people seem to assume it is their role to question everything the elders do. Sometimes they decide that their leaders

> Leaders will not always get it right—but do not assume you would do better.

have made a good decision, and sometimes they complain that their leaders have made a bad decision. But here's what they are doing: they are assuming that they know best. They are the all-knowing ones who should judge whether leaders are making good decisions or not. They're sitting in authority, in their own hearts, over their elders— as though there is a category above the God-given leaders in their church, and the one person in that category of authority is... them. If that is true, then they should be leading instead of the leaders God has placed over their church!

Sometimes people question pastoral actions, even when they do not know all the facts. And the problem is that often leaders cannot explain why they have done something because they do not want publicly to shame people or reveal confidences. You would not want everyone being told about *your* issues. It is quite common for leaders to find themselves accused of handling a situation badly. Perhaps someone has given a plausible justification of themselves, and the only way a leader can defend themselves is to dish the dirt on someone else. That is not something they should be forced to do. Make it your default position to trust your leaders in those situations.

When it comes to grumbling or gossip, we should be a buffer, not a channel. When you hear grumbling or gossip, you should act like one of those huge buffers at the end of train tracks that stop trains careering on, out of control, with a crash inevitable further ahead. Stop gossip and complaining in its tracks. Bounce it back to the source. If someone comes with a complaint about the leaders—or anyone else—tell them to sort it out with the person concerned.

There is simply no need for constant questioning. It is "warped and sinful" (**3:11**). Instead, let's spend our time and energy, and allow others to spend their time and energy, stressing the kindness and love of God. I sometimes see letters or emails people have written and think: *How long did this take you? You could have spent that time doing something "profitable". You could have been stressing the kindness and love of God to some weary saint or lost soul instead of pursuing controversies and arguments that are "useless".*

No Room for Ministry Competitiveness

We get a glimpse of the attitude Paul is commending in the personal remarks with which he ends the letter. Paul wants to send Artemas or Tychicus to Crete, so that they can replace Titus in order for him to join Paul for a time (**v 12**). And then in **verse 13**, Paul says: "Do everything you can to help Zenas the lawyer and Apollos on their way and see that they have everything they need". We do not know anything about Zenas; but the Apollos mentioned here is probably the Apollos described in 1 Corinthians 1:11-12 and 3:1-9, who was seen by some as a rival to Paul. It seems that some of the Christians in the church in

Corinth preferred the ministry of Apollos, while others liked the minis- try of Paul: "One says, 'I follow Paul,' and another, 'I follow Apollos'" (1 Corinthians 3:4). *Paul, if only you were more like Apollos. Paul, you should learn from Apollos. We love to follow Apollos.*

So here is a man who is being exalted above, and against, Paul's ministry by Christians in churches Paul had planted. With this going on, it would be easy for Paul to feel competitive about Apollos, and bitter towards him. How easy for him to want to undermine Apol- los—at best, surely he would focus on his own ministry rather than that of the man whom others are holding up as some kind of rival to him and example for him?

But this is not how Paul sees it (and presumably not how Apollos sees it either). Paul and Apollos are only servants. Jesus is the one who is the Lord, says Paul in 1 Corinthians 3, and God is one who makes the church grow. If this is the same Apollos, then the lack of rivalry between those co-workers is evidenced in Paul's concern that Titus do all he can to meet the needs of Zenas and Apollos. There will be no divisiveness here—Apollos must have everything he needs to continue to stress the gospel, for the glory of God.

Questions for reflection

1. Do you find it easy to discuss controversy instead of the gospel? When? And how could you make sure you focus on the gospel in that situation next time?

2. How seriously do you view divisiveness?

3. Are you ever tempted to stand in judgment over your church lead- ers? What needs to change?

PART TWO

Doing Good

Paul summarises the gospel in verses 3-7 so that we might "stress these things" (**v 8**). But talking about the gospel among ourselves is not an end in itself. "Stress these things, so that…" Here is the reason why we are to stress these things: "so that those who have trusted in God may be careful to devote themselves to doing what is good".

This emphasis on doing good is there at the beginning of the chapter, in **verse 1**: "Remind the people to be subject to rulers and authorities, to be obedient, to be ready to do whatever is good." It is there in **verse 8**, in the middle of the chapter. And it comes again at the end of the chapter, in **verse 14**: "Our people must learn to devote themselves to doing what is good, in order that they may provide for daily necessities and not live unproductive lives."

In fact, this concern for doing good runs through the whole letter. Jesus "gave himself for us to purify for himself a people that are his very own, eager to do what is good" (2:14). The false teachers are unfit for doing anything good (1:16), but Titus is to set: "an example by doing what is good" (2:7).

We are to stress the gospel so that we live the gospel. We are stress the good God has done to us so that we do good to other people. The trustworthy saying of 3:4-7 is written to encourage missional involvement in the world.

Being Subject

Paul says Christians should be "subject to rulers and authorities" (**v 1**). That was not an easy proposition for the church in Crete. The Greek historian Polybius said it was:

"impossible to find … personal conduct more treacherous or public policy more unjust than in Crete."

(cited in William D. Mounce, *Pastoral Epistles*, page 444)

Nor is Paul commending (or commanding) mere passive **acquiescence**. In contrast to the false teachers, who are "unfit for doing anything good" (1:16), people shaped by the gospel are to "be ready to do whatever is good" (**3:1**). According to both Paul and Peter, the state has a negative and a positive duty: to punish evil and to promote good (Romans 13:4; 1 Peter 2:14). And Christians have a corresponding double duty: to submit and to do good. We are to be people who are proactively looking for opportunities to bless our cities and to serve our neighbours.

Humility and Gentleness

Titus **3:2** begins with a call to "slander no one", and ends with a call to be "gentle towards everyone". "Always to be gentle towards everyone" is literally to be "all gentleness to all people". In other words, these exhortations encompass all people and all of life. There are two negatives and two positives:

- don't slander

- don't quarrel (this is the literal rendering of "be peaceable")

- be considerate

- be gentle

The words for the two positive virtues ("considerate" and "gentle") are used by Paul to describe Jesus in 2 Corinthians 10:1: "By the humility and gentleness of Christ, I appeal to you..." We are to treat people the way Jesus treated people.

As we saw in the last chapter, this is radically different from how the world around us works; and how we once worked, because: "At one time we too were foolish" (Titus **3:3**). We live in a world of people who are foolish, disobedient, deceived, enslaved, living in malice and envy, hating and hated. So it is very tempting to withdraw from that world, or to look down on that world. Christians can find unbelievers scary. We find it much more comfortable spending our time with fellow Christians. Meanwhile we tell one another our stories of the appalling behaviour of people in the big, bad world outside. But Paul says: *That's what you were like, too—and it is only grace that saved you from that and keeps you from that.* We have no basis for feeling smug or superior. This is what we were like.

If you try to be peaceable, considerate and gentle, what you often receive in return is the malice, envy and hatred of the world. What do you do when that happens? You remember what you used to be like. What did God do when you hated him? He did not stand at a distance; and neither should we. He did not stay safe. He appeared; he entered our world in kindness and mercy. In the same way, we "appear"—we get involved in the world with kindness and mercy, even when that comes at a cost to ourselves. We cannot say: *I want to keep myself pure so I need to keep myself away. I want to protect my family, so I will keep them out of the world.* God did not say that—if he had, his Son would never have come and saved us. When Paul says we are to "be ready to do whatever is good" (**v 1**) and are "to devote [ourselves] to doing what is good" (**v 8, 14**), he is encouraging (or forcing) us to engage with the world, to seek to bless the world, even when the world throws it back at us.

> God did not stand at a distance; and neither should we.

All the way through this letter, Paul says Christians must live in the world in a way that commends Jesus. It is true in the home. Younger women are "to be self-controlled and pure, to be busy at home, to be kind, and to be subject to their husbands, so that no one will malign the word of God" (2:5). And it is true in the workplace. Slaves are "to be subject to their masters in everything, to try to please them, not to talk back to them, and not to steal from them, but to show that they can be fully trusted, so that in every way they will make the teaching about God our Saviour attractive" (2:9-10).

In both the home and in the workplace, we are to live in a way that commends Christ. In other words, we do mission in the context of everyday life. There is a place for special events and evangelistic courses. But the bedrock of mission is doing good in everyday life: in your home, on your street, in your workplace, in your school, in your neighbourhood. We stress the gospel to each other so that we will live the gospel in front of others.

What is it that inspires and energises and motivates and shapes this everyday mission? It is the kindness and love of God. "I want you to stress these things, so that those who have trusted in God may be careful to devote themselves to doing what is good" (**3:8**).

Good Life = Missional Life

Roy Hattersley is the former deputy leader of the Labour Party in the UK and a public atheist (as the following quote makes clear). Here he writes about his experience of joining Christians from the Salvation Army one evening as they cared for those in need on the streets.

"The arguments against religion are well known and persuasive ... Yet men and women who believe ... are the people most likely to take the risks and make the sacrifices involved in helping others ... Good works, John Wesley [the 18th-century evangelist and founder of the Methodist Church] insisted, are no guarantee of a place in heaven. But they are most likely to be performed by people who believe that heaven exists. The correlation is so clear that it is impossible to doubt that faith and charity go hand in hand ... It ought to be possible to live a Christian life without being a Christian ... Yet men and women who, like me, cannot accept the mysteries and the miracles do not go out with the Salvation Army at night.

"The only possible conclusion is that faith comes with a packet of moral imperatives that, while they do not condition the attitude of all believers, influence enough of them to make them morally superior to atheists like me. The truth may make us free. But it has not made us as admirable as the average captain in the Salvation Army."

Titus is to teach the church in Crete to live in such a way that "no one will malign the word of God" (2:5). We are to live that way today, too. People like Roy Hattersley may not be persuaded by our arguments, but they cannot refute the evidence of our lives.

Maybe it is my old age, but more than ever I feel a sense of threat from the world around us. People are cynical. They mistrust authority. You do not obey the law; you just obey the laws that are enforced. You get away with what you can get away with. People readily criticise others or put them down. They are quick to argue, to threaten, and to fight. They are often inconsiderate and selfish. They will cut you up on the roads and drop litter in the street. There is a harshness about life. I used to drive to work each day, and hardly a day would go by without me witnessing some kind of impatience or anger from other road users. A few weeks ago, a member of our church collapsed in her local supermarket. She was nine months pregnant. Yet, as she sat on the floor, people ignored her. No one came to help.

We live in a harsh, selfish, uncaring culture. In this context, listen again to the words of Titus **3:1-2**: "Remind the people to be subject to rulers and authorities, to be obedient, to be ready to do whatever is good, to slander no one, to be peaceable and considerate, and always to be gentle towards everyone." Imagine a community within our society that is subject to authorities, obedient, and ready to do whatever is good. A community that slanders no one, which is peaceable and considerate, and which shows gentleness to all people without discrimination. That community would commend the kindness and love of God our Saviour. That community would shine

> Imagine a community that is considerate and gentle to all without discrimination.

like stars as it held to the word of life and held out the word of life (Philippians 2:14-16).

That is what the community of Christ's people on Crete is to be, Paul tells Titus. He ends with a conventional closing greeting, but notably uses "you" plural in his last line: "Grace to you all" (Titus **3:15**). This way of life is for church leaders; but it is not just for them, because grace has come to every church member. Each member of their community should shine like stars; and every member of our communities of Christ's people should, too. As we "learn to devote [ourselves] to doing what is good", we will "not live unproductive lives" (**v 14**). No—we will live the gospel life, the good life, the missional life.

Questions for reflection

1. How are you living in a humble and gentle way? How could you do so increasingly?

2. Do you ever do the godly thing, only to be met with malice or envy? How do these verses encourage you to keep going?

3. How will the gospel motivate you to live productively today?

GLOSSARY

Acquiescence: agreeing to something by not resisting it happening; giving way.

Allusion: a reference to something else.

Antinomianism: the belief that Christians are not required to keep the moral law.

Atrophies: wastes away.

Authenticates: shows something is genuine.

Catharsis: the release of repressed emotions.

Converted: become a Christian.

Disciples: people who follow Jesus as Lord and trust him as Saviour.

Discipling: helping people to know God better, follow Jesus more closely and grow in their faith.

Doctrine: the study of what is true about God.

Elect: those to whom God has chosen to give saving faith, so that they become Christians.

Excommunication: to exclude someone from the church, so that they are no longer recognised as a member of the church.

Exhortation: strong urging or encouragement.

Gentiles: people who are not ethnically Jewish.

Gospel: an announcement, often translated "good news". When the Roman Emperor sent a proclamation around the empire declaring a victory or achievement, this was called a "gospel". The gospel is good news to be believed, not good advice to be followed. **Gospel ministry** is the work of proclaiming the gospel to people (both Christians and non-believers).

Grace: unmerited favour. In the Bible, "grace" is usually used to describe how God treats his people. Because God is full of grace, he gives believers eternal life (Ephesians 2:4-8); he also gives them gifts to use to serve his people (Ephesians 4:7, 11-13).

Heretic: someone who, despite being challenged, continues to hold to a belief which directly opposes the biblical gospel.

Incarnation: the coming of the divine Son of God as a human, in the person of Jesus Christ.

Incredulity: being unwilling to believe something.

Instigation: to instigate an event is to bring it about.

Insubordinate: defiant towards or disobedient of someone who has the right to be in authority.

Intentionality: being deliberate.

Malice: the desire to do evil.

Manifested: made clear.

Manifold: many and various. The Greek word literally means "many-coloured".

Missional: something that communicates or promotes the gospel message to non-Christians.

Orthodoxy: standard, accepted Christian teaching.

Pagan: people who don't know and worship the true God.

Parity: equality.

Pentecost: a Jewish feast celebrating God giving his people his law on Mount Sinai (Exodus 19 – 31). On the day of this feast, fifty days after Jesus' resurrection, the Holy Spirit came to the first Christians (Acts 2), so "Pentecost" is how Christians tend to refer to this event.

Redemption: the act of redeeming, or releasing, sinners. In Paul's time, one could redeem a slave by paying their owner the full price for their release. By dying on the cross, Jesus paid the penalty for sin to release Christians from slavery to sin, death and judgment (see Romans 3:23-25; Ephesians 1:7).

Reformer: one of the first two generations of people in the fifteenth and early-sixteenth centuries who preached the gospel of justification by faith, and opposed the Pope and the Roman church.

Repent, repentance: literally, a military word meaning "about turn". Used to mean turning around to live the opposite way to previously.

Refute: prove a statement or theory to be wrong.

Slanderers: people who make false and damaging accusations against others.

Sovereignty: supreme authority / being the supreme ruler.

Testimony: evidence or claims about Jesus.

Trinitarian: relating to the biblical doctrine of the Trinity—that the one God is three Persons, distinct from one another, each fully God, of the same "essence" (or "God-ness"). We usually call these three Persons Father, Son and Holy Spirit.

BIBLIOGRAPHY

- John Calvin, *Commentary on Timothy, Titus, Philemon* (Christian Classics Ethereal Library, 1999)

- Gordon D. Fee, *1 and 2 Timothy, Titus* in the New International Commentary series (Hendrickson, 1984)

- J. N. D. Kelly, *The Pastoral Epistles* in Black's New Testament Commentary series (Hendrickson, 1960)

- George W. Knight III, *The Pastoral Epistles* in the The New International Greek Commentary series (Eerdmans/Paternoster, 1992)

- William D. Mounce, *Pastoral Epistles* in the Word Biblical Commentary series, Volume 46 (Thomas Nelson, 2000)

- John Stott, *The Message of 1 Timothy and Titus* in The Bible Speaks Today series (IVP, 1996)

Titus for...
Bible-study Groups

Tim Chester's **Good Book Guide** to Titus is the companion to this resource, helping groups of Christians to explore, discuss and apply the book together. Five studies, each including investigation, apply, getting personal, pray and explore more sections, take you through the book of Titus. Includes a concise Leader's Guide at the back.

Find out more at:
www.thegoodbook.com/goodbookguides

Daily Devotionals

Explore daily devotional helps you open up the Scriptures and will encourage and equip you in your walk with God. Available as a quarterly booklet, *Explore* is also available as an app, where you can download notes on Titus, as well as Tim Chester's notes on various Bible books. Other contributors include Timothy Keller, Mark Dever, Mike McKinley, Mark Meynell, Stephen Witmer and Ray Ortlund.

Find out more at:
www.thegoodbook.com/explore

More For You

Judges For You *Timothy Keller*

"Our era can be characterised by the phrase: 'Everyone did as he saw fit' (Judges 21:25). So the book of Judges has much to say to the individualism and paganism of our own day. And it has much to say about the God of grace, who works in the worst of situations, and who triumphs over the stupidest of actions."

Romans 1-7 For You *Timothy Keller*

"Reading Romans, we should be prepared to have our hearts shaped and lives changed by God's gift of righteousness. It will prompt us to ask: *Have I, as Martin Luther put it, 'broken through' into the freedom and release the gospel brings me, both in terms of my future and right now?*"

The Whole Series

- **Exodus For You**
  Tim Chester
- **Judges For You**
  Timothy Keller
- **Ruth For You**
  Tony Merida
- **1 Samuel For You**
  Tim Chester
- **2 Samuel For You**
  Tim Chester
- **Psalms For You**
  Christopher Ash
- **Proverbs For You**
  Kathleen Nielson
- **Daniel For You**
  David Helm
- **Micah For You**
  Stephen Um
- **Luke 1-12 For You**
  Mike McKinley
- **Luke 12-24 For You**
  Mike McKinley
- **John 1-12 For You**
  Josh Moody
- **John 13-21 For You**
  Josh Moody
- **Acts 1-12 For You**
  Albert Mohler

- **Acts 13-28 For You**
  Albert Mohler
- **Romans 1-7 For You**
  Timothy Keller
- **Romans 8-16 For You**
  Timothy Keller
- **2 Corinthians For You**
  Gary Millar
- **Galatians For You**
  Timothy Keller
- **Ephesians For You**
  Richard Coekin
- **Philippians For You**
  Steven Lawson
- **Colossians & Philemon For You**
  Mark Meynell
- **1 & 2 Timothy For You**
  Phillip Jensen
- **Titus For You**
  Tim Chester
- **James For You**
  Sam Allberry
- **1 Peter For You**
  Juan Sanchez
- **Revelation For You**
  Tim Chester

Find out more about these resources at:
www.thegoodbook.com/for-you